Contents

As we live in a rapidly changing society, exposure to and fluency in Science, Technology, Engineering, and Mathematics (STEM) ensures students will gain the skills they will need to succeed in the 21st century. Its essential that students gain practice in becoming good problem solvers, critical thinkers, innovators, inventors, and risk-takers.

Teacher Tips

Encourage Topic Interest

Help students develop an understanding and appreciation of different STEM concepts by providing an area in the classroom to display topic-related non-fiction books, pictures, collections, and artifacts as a springboard for learning.

What I Think I Know/What I Would Like to Know Activity

Introduce each STEM unit by asking students what they think they know about the topic, and what they would like to know about the topic. Complete this activity as a whole-group brainstorming session, in cooperative small groups, or independently. Once students have had a chance to complete the questions, combine the information to create a class chart for display. Throughout the study, periodically update students' progress in accomplishing their goal of what they want to know, and validate what they think they know.

Vocabulary List

Keep track of new and theme-related vocabulary on chart paper for students' reference. Encourage students to add theme-related words. Classify the word list into the categories of nouns, verbs, and adjectives. In addition, have students create their own science dictionaries as part of their learning logs.

Learning Logs

Keeping a learning log is an effective way for students to organize thoughts and ideas about the STEM concepts presented and examined. Students' learning logs also provide insight on what follow-up activities are needed to review and to clarify concepts learned.

Learning logs can include the following types of entries:

- Teacher prompts
- Students' personal reflections
- Questions that arise
- Connections discovered
- Labeled diagrams and pictures
- Definitions for new vocabulary

Your Respiratory System

In and out, in and out. You do not even think about it, but you breathe constantly. You have to, since breathing brings in the oxygen your cells need to work. Breathing also takes away the carbon dioxide that the cells produce.

The Respiratory Route

When you breathe in, air enters your nose and mouth and flows into your nasal cavity. There, it is warmed and cleaned. Air then flows down the main part of your throat, or pharynx, to your larynx which contains your vocal cords. Then air enters the trachea, or windpipe, which branches into two bronchial tubes—one leading to each lung. Those tubes branch into many smaller tubes called bronchioles. Your lungs are at the end of this system of tubes.

Oxygen In, Carbon Dioxide Out

At the end of the bronchioles are bundles of air sacs called alveoli. There, your blood picks up the oxygen you breathe in and drops off the carbon dioxide you breathe out.

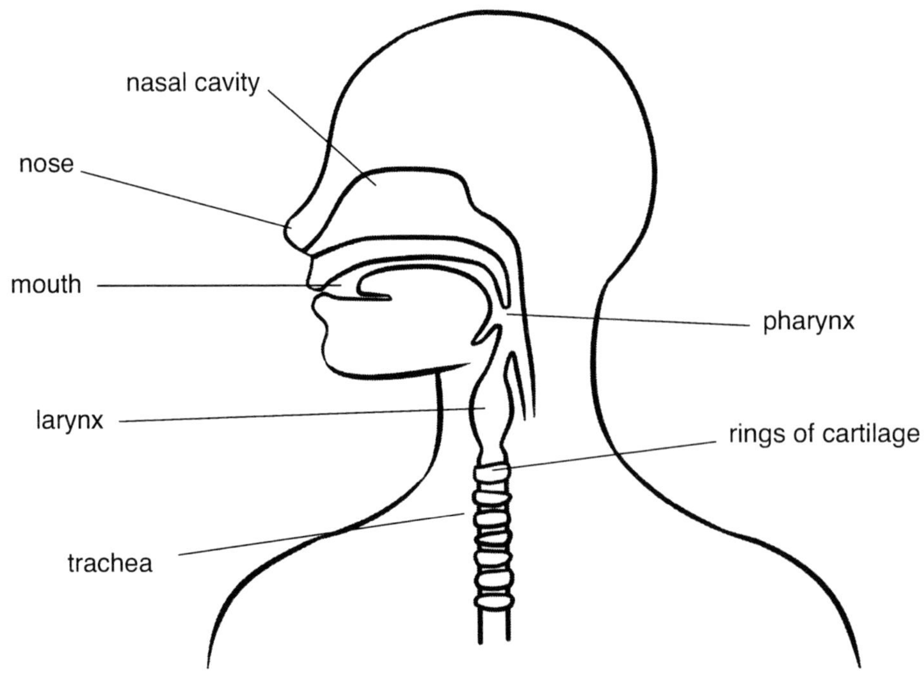

Lung Action

You have two lungs: right and left.

Under the lungs is a muscle called the diaphragm. When this muscle pulls down, your lungs expand and fill with air. You breathe in. When the diaphragm relaxes, air is pushed out of the lungs. You breath out. When you are just sitting, you breathe about 20 times each minute. That number can double when you are running.

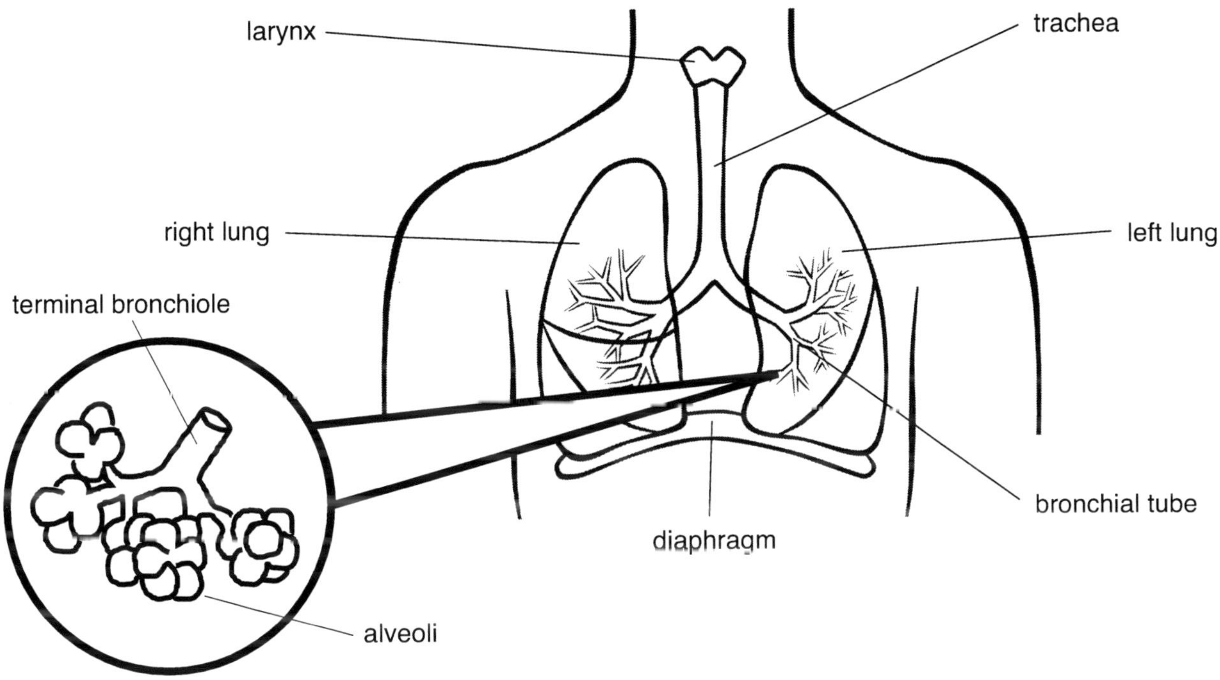

Sticky and Slimy

In your nose, mucous glands produce that slimy substance. Mucus keeps your nose moist, and traps dirt and germs. It helps keep you healthy.

Feel Those Rings

Your trachea is made of rings of firm, flexible cartilage. You can run your fingertips up and down the front of your neck to feel these rings.

Up in Smoke

Healthy lungs are pink and clean. But the lungs of a smoker are dark gray and full of dirt. That is because chemicals in cigarette smoke damage the trachea. It can no longer keep the dirt out. Also, the smallest tubes in the lungs fill up with tar from the cigarettes. Because of this, a smoker's lungs do not work well and make breathing difficult.

"Your Respiratory System"—Think About It!

1. The diagram below shows the route air takes when we breathe. (White arrows show inhaling, and dark arrows show exhaling.) Complete the diagram by naming parts of the respiratory system.

a) The two places where we inhale and exhale: ________________ and ________________

b) The space in the nose where air is warmed and cleaned: ____________________________

c) The main part of the throat: ______________________________

d) The tube in the throat that contains the vocal cords: ______________________________

e) What directs air into the right or left lung: __________________________________

f) Small air passages at the ends of the bronchial tubes: ______________________________

g) Where oxygen is added to blood and carbon dioxide is removed: ______________________

2. List ways your respiratory system can be affected when you have a cold.

____

____

____

____

____

____

Experiment: How Much Air?

How much air is in a single breath you take? Try this experiment to find out.

What You Need

- Sink or large bowl
- Water
- Bendable straw
- 2-L plastic soda bottle with cap
- Measuring cup
- Partner

What You Do

1. Completely fill the soda bottle with water and screw on the cap. Then fill the sink or bowl with water until it is about half full.
2. Turn the bottle upside down and hold it in the water so the cap is underwater. Remove the cap while it is underwater. Make sure no air gets inside the bottle.
3. Have your partner hold the bottle for you. Place one end of the straw in the opening of the bottle. Take a deep breath and blow into the straw. The air you blow out will go into the bottle.
4. While your partner holds the top of the bottle underwater, screw on the cap.

5. Lift the bottle out of the water. Turn it upright and remove the cap. Fill the measuring cup with water. (Do not use the water from the bottle.) Record how much water is in the measuring cup.
6. Slowly pour water from the measuring cup into the bottle until it is full. Look at the markings on the measuring cup. Check how much water it took to fill the bottle.
7. Repeat the experiment, letting your partner blow air into the bottle this time.

Think About It!

1. How much water did it take to refill the bottle?

   You: ______________________ Your partner: ______________________

2. What was the amount (volume) of water you poured into the bottle in step 6? What volume of air did you breathe into the bottle in step 3? Explain why the volumes are the same.

   ____

   ____

   ____

Your Circulatory System

The circulatory system delivers food and oxygen to your body's cells. These fuels are carried in your blood. Blood takes waste to your kidneys. It also transports messenger chemicals throughout your body.

Have a Heart

Your heart is a muscle about the size of your fist. Blood enters the heart, then gets pumped to the lungs to pick up oxygen. Blood also drops off carbon dioxide in your lungs. This blood then goes back through the heart, where it is pumped throughout your body.

In just one day, your heart beats about 100,000 times. It pumps 2,008 gal (7,600 L) of blood every day. The heart is a very hard-working muscle.

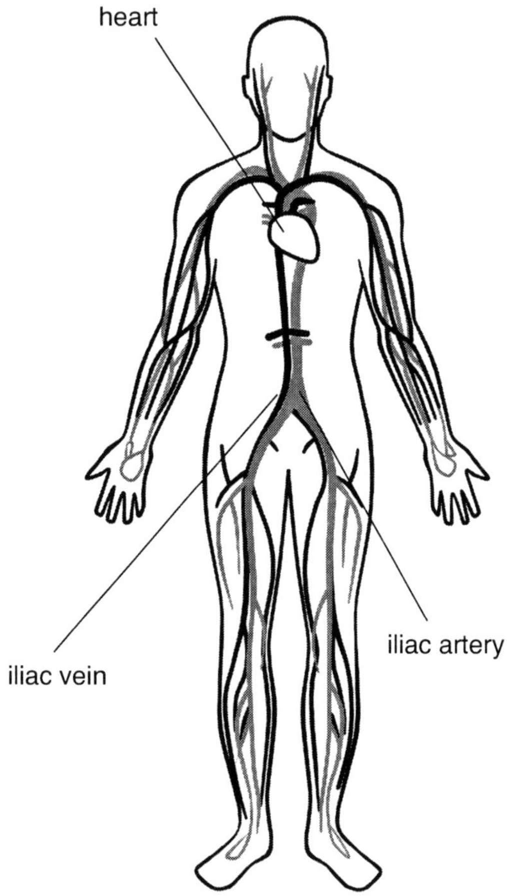

Blood Vessels

Blood vessels are tubes that transport your blood. Arteries carry oxygen-rich blood away from the heart to the cells of your body. Your veins carry the oxygen-poor blood from those cells back to the heart.

This network would be about 62,137 mi (100,000 km) long, stretched out.

That Amazing Red Stuff

The body of an average adult contains 5 qt (5 L) of blood. Each droplet carries food, chemicals, waste, and billions of blood cells throughout your body.

In each drop of blood:

375,000 white blood cells fight germs and infections
13,000,000 platelets help your blood form scabs
250,000,000 red blood cells carry the oxygen cells need

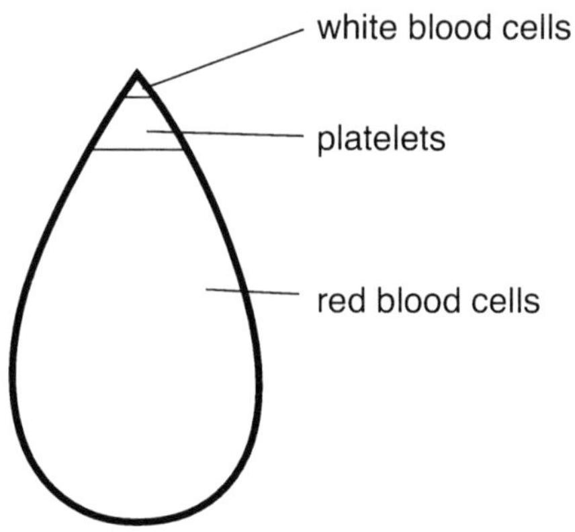

"Your Circulatory System"—Think About It!

1. Count Your Pulse Rate

Each time your heart beats, blood flows through your arteries. The arteries swell slightly as blood flows through them. This temporary swelling is called a pulse. You can feel it in places where your arteries are close to your skin. Two places to feel your pulse are your wrist and neck.

Find out what your pulse rate is. Place a finger on the inside of your wrist. Do not use your thumb. Can you feel a beat? Count your pulse for one minute.

a) My resting pulse is ______________________________ beats per minute.

Jog on the spot or run outside for a few minutes. Then take your pulse.

b) My active pulse is ______________________________ beats per minute.

c) Which number is higher? ___________________________

2. Multiple Pulses

Place two fingers of your right hand on the right side of your neck. Place them just below your jaw. You will feel a pulse as your carotid artery carries blood to your head.

Keep your fingers on your neck. Place the fingers of your left hand on your right wrist to feel the pulse there.

a) Focus on the two pulses you can feel. Which pulse is stronger?

____

b) Which pulse can you feel first?

____

c) How can you explain these results?

____

____

____

____

Your Digestive System

Oxygen is an important fuel for your body, and so is food. Food gives your body's cells energy to breathe, move, and do many other things. Food also provides your body with proteins, vitamins, and minerals.

Take a Bite

Digestion starts when you take a bite of food. The food is ground up and wetted. Then your tongue pushes it back to your esophagus which squeezes it down to your stomach.

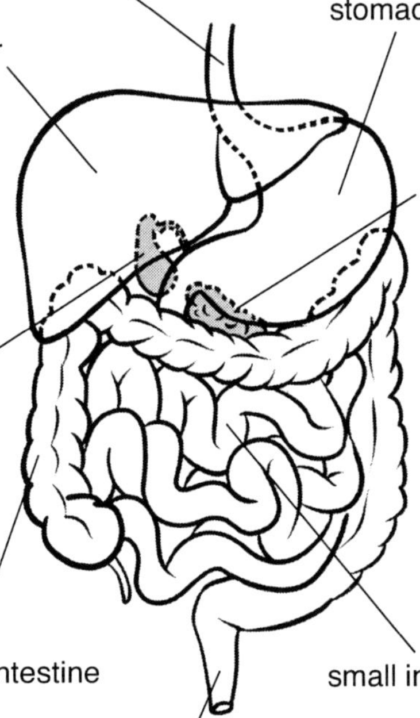

Down in the Stomach

Your stomach is a big bag where the food gets broken down. The muscles in your stomach squeeze the food. Digestive juices dissolve the food. They are made in your liver, pancreas, and gall bladder.

Your Two Intestines

From your stomach, the food moves into a crooked tube called the small intestine. This is where the nutrients are extracted from the food. Anything left over moves down into the large intestine or colon. Here, water is soaked up and the waste is formed into lumps.

Taking Out the Garbage

The leftover waste then moves into your excretory system. Extra water, or urine, goes into the bladder. It is stored there until you go to the toilet. Solid waste leaves your body through a tube called the rectum.

"Your Digestive System"—Think About It!

1. List, from first to last, the organs food passes through in your digestive system.

   small intestine   rectum   stomach   esophagus   large intestine   mouth

   a) ______________________ d) ______________________

   b) ______________________ e) ______________________

   c) ______________________ f) ______________________

2. Which of the organs listed in question 1 are tubes? Circle them in the list.

3. How could you make a model of the digestive system? Write a list of materials you could use. Match each material to a part of the digestive system. If there is time, work with a group to build the model.

4. **Touch a Tooth:** Your teeth are an important part of your digestive system. Wash your hands carefully. Then feel the shapes of your teeth.

   a) Which teeth would be good for biting pieces off an apple? Why do you think so?

   b) Which teeth would be good for crushing food? Explain.

Your Bones and Skeleton

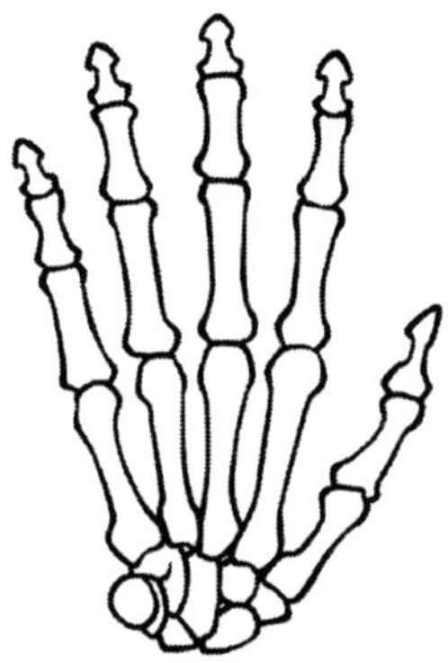

Adults have 206 bones. Each hand has 27 bones and each foot has 26.

Bones have many shapes. Your 12 pairs of ribs are curved. They form a protective cage around your chest. There is a straight bone running down each leg from the hip to the knee. This thigh bone is the longest bone in your body. Your body's smallest bone is in the ear. It is shaped like a stirrup on a horse's saddle.

Down at the Corner

Bones connect to other bones at joints. You have about 360 joints, including your knees, elbows, and hips. Cartilage is a tough, flexible tissue. It covers the ends of bones in joints. Cartilage also shapes your nose and ears.

Joints are held together by ligaments. Ligaments are straps of strong, flexible tissue. There are different types of joints in your body because they have different jobs to do. They also have to move in different ways. For example, your knee is a hinge joint. It moves like a hinge on a door.

Think About It!

1. Look at the types of joints shown below. Move your body. Can you find joints on your body that might look like these? Write your ideas.

a) Hinge joint 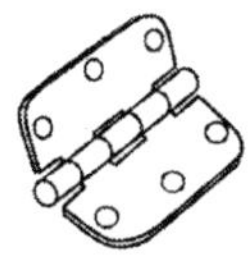 ______________________________

b) Ball and socket joint  ______________________________

c) Pivot joint 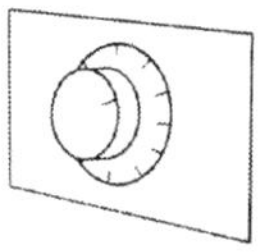 ______________________________

2. Give an example of how bones support your body.

____

3. How do bones protect your body? Give an example.

____

4. How do bones and joints help you move? Explain.

____

____

The Muscles of Your Body

Your bones and joints need muscles to help them move. There are about 660 muscles in your body. Skeletal muscles shape the body and hold it upright.

Another important muscle is your diaphragm. It is a dome-shaped muscle below your lungs. This muscle squeezes your lungs when you breathe out. Muscles in your intestines work without you thinking about them.

Pulling in Pairs

Muscles can only pull bones and joints, they cannot push them. So muscles often work in pairs. For example, the bicep muscle bends your arm. Your tricep muscle straightens your arm. It does this by pulling on the back of your elbow. Touch your arm and you will feel them working.

Tough Tendons

Each muscle narrows into a cord at the end. This is dense, tough tissue known as a tendon. Tendons are attached to bones. When the muscle contracts, the tendon pulls on the bone.

The jaw muscle is the strongest muscle in your body. Your tongue is a muscle that helps you communicate, and eat. It takes about 16 muscles to smile.

"The Muscles of Your Body"—Think About It!

1. a) List at least four occupations in which having strong muscles is important. Justify your thinking.

____

____

____

b) List three ways muscles are used by people who work at a desk all day. Justify your thinking.

____

____

____

2. Which muscle helps you breathe? ______________________________

____

____

3. Which muscles bend your arms? ______________________________

____

____

4. Which muscles straighten your arms? ______________________________

____

____

5. Which muscle pumps your blood? ______________________________

____

____

Touch a Tendon

You can feel your Achilles tendon. It is one of the largest tendons in your body. Pinch your lower leg, just above your heel. The tendon feels hard like a bone. But when you press it, it bends slightly. The Achilles tendon joins the muscles in your calf to your heel. This is so you can pull up your foot when you walk.

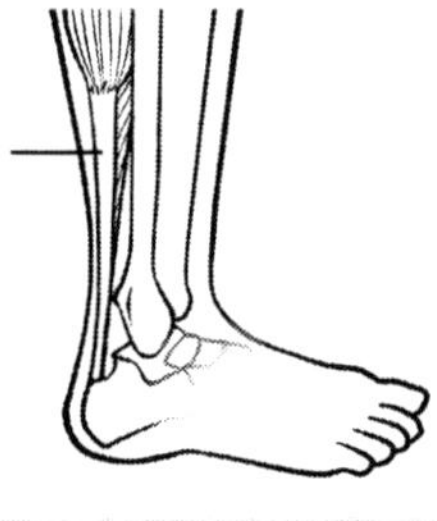
Achilles tendon

Your Nervous System

Feeling, seeing, hearing, moving, thinking. You can do all of these things at the same time, thanks to your nervous system. It is the control center of your body. It automatically regulates many of your body's processes.

The Brains Behind the Operation

The central nervous system is made up of your brain and spinal cord. They are linked to your body through a network of nerve cells.

Nerves use electricity and chemicals to transmit messages. These messages go to and from your brain.

Making Sense

You have five senses: sight, hearing, smell, taste, and touch. Your eyes, ears, nose, mouth, and skin all send messages to your brain. The brain processes the messages and allows you to sense and react to your environment.

Your five senses communicate with your brain while you eat a snow cone.

A Matter of Survival

Your nervous system is important for your survival. For example, if you touch something hot, you quickly move your hand away. That reaction is automatic—a reflex. If you see a car racing toward you, your eyes send a message to your brain. Your brain delivers a message to your feet to start running.

Your Amazing Nervous System

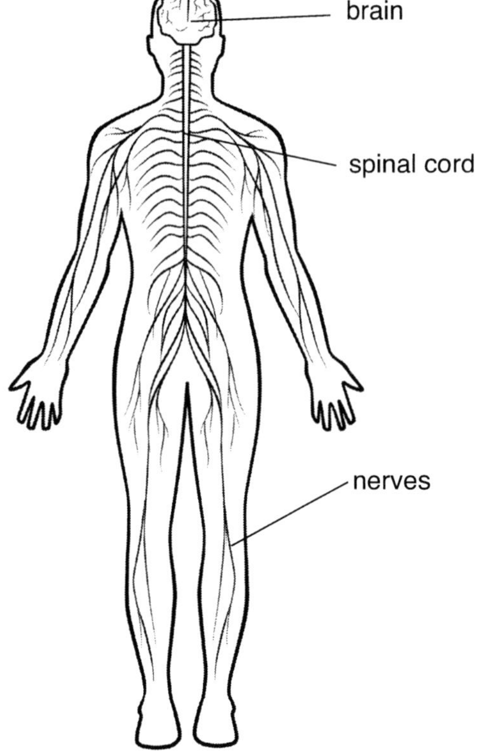

There are thousands of miles (kilometers) of nerves in your body. Laid out end to end, your nerves would wrap around Earth twice! Nerves carry messages at the speed of up to 267 mph (430 km/h).

There are neurons that run from your spinal cord to your toes. They are the longest cells in your body. They are incredibly narrow, but are up to 4 ft (1.2 m) long.

Think About It!

1. Write a decription about the work your nerves did during a game you played. Use the information you read and your own ideas. (**Hint:** Remember your body as well as your senses.)

___

___

___

___

Feed Your Brain

You sleep and do not eat during the night. Your brain needs fuel when you wake up. Experts have shown that "hungry" brains have trouble remembering things. They also have trouble learning new information. So do your brain a favor—eat breakfast! Protein foods are very good "brain foods" for breakfast. Protein foods include eggs and nuts. Oatmeal cereal and whole-grain bread are also good breakfast foods.

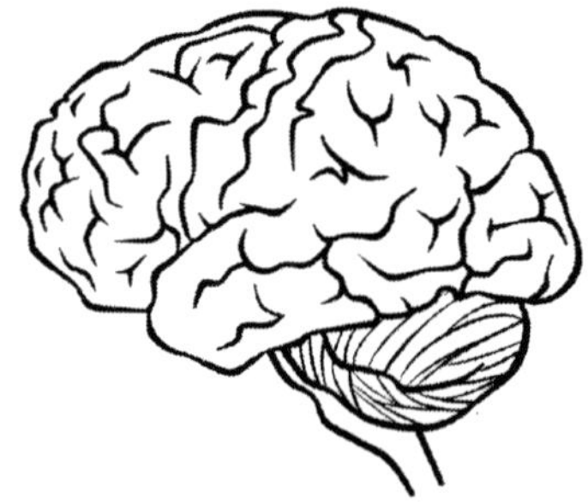

Experiment 1: Test Your Reflexes

Here is a simple experiment to test your reflexes. You will need a ruler and a partner.

1. Hold the ruler near the end with the highest number and let the ruler hang down. Have your partner put his or her hand at the bottom of the ruler. Your partner should get ready to grab the ruler. But they should not be touching the ruler.
2. Tell your partner that you will drop the ruler soon. Your partner should grab the ruler as soon as possible after you drop it. Record the level in inches (centimeters) where he or she catches the ruler. Try the experiment a few times, changing how soon you drop the ruler. Then switch roles and try it again.

   The smaller the number of inches (centimeters), the faster your reflexes. What happens when you repeat the experiment a number of times? Can you catch the ruler more quickly? Try the experiment in dim light. Record your results. Are your reflexes faster or slower?

Experiment 2: Find Your Blind Spot

You may think your vision is pretty good, but did you know you have a blind spot? That is a place where you cannot see anything. Normally you do not notice your blind spot. Here is an experiment to help you find it.

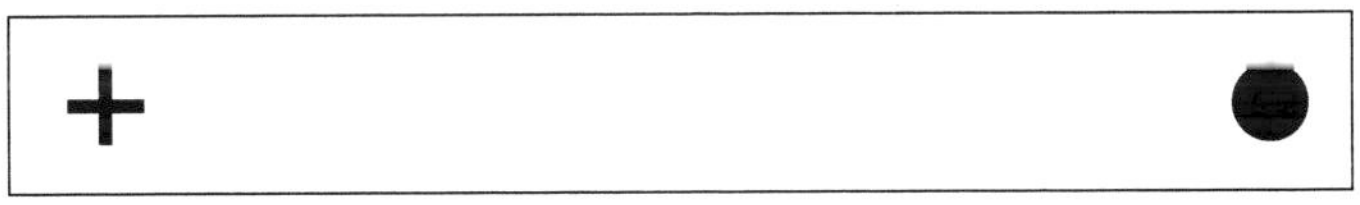

1. Close your right eye and hold this page at arm's length.
2. Look at the dot with your left eye. You should also be able to see the plus sign.
3. Move the page slowly toward you. The plus sign will disappear at a certain point.

You can test your right eye by closing your left eye. Then focus on the plus sign.

What is happening? Blood vessels and a major nerve pass through a place at the back of your eyeball. Millions of cells in your eyes receive images and send information to your brain. But there are no cells at that particular place, so you have a blind spot.

Experiment 3: Trick Your Brain

Cross the index and middle finger of one hand. Now touch your nose with your crossed fingertips. For most people, it feels as though they have two noses. Why do you think this is?

Overview of the Human __________ System

Write a description of this system.
List the parts of the body that make up this system.
How do these parts work together?
How does the body use this system?

Sunlight and Vitamin D

You have to make decisions about how to keep your body fit. You decide what to eat and how to get enough exercise. You may also decide to stay out of the sun and not allow your skin to burn.

Skin cancer caused by being out in the sun too much is a health concern. But people need sunlight to make vitamin D. How can you get enough of this nutrient without damaging your skin?

Why You Need Vitamin D

Vitamin D helps bones grow and stay strong. Calcium and other minerals are stored in bones. Your bones need vitamin D to absorb these minerals properly.

Why Do People Not Get Enough Vitamin D?

Your body makes a lot of vitamin D when it gets sunlight. People may avoid sunlight to protect their skin. Where you live can also make it difficult to get vitamin D from sunlight. Why? You may have to cover up to be warm or to cool off. Also, sunlight gets weaker as you move away from the equator. So people who live far from the equator do not get enough vitamin D.

Sunscreen also reduces the amount of sunlight your skin receives. Sunscreen with an SPF of 15 can block 99 percent of you body's vitamin D production.

Brain Stretch

On a separate piece of paper, draft a persuasive radio commercial to promote the benefits of vitamin D. Share it with your class. Use this checklist to help you:

- ☐ My commercial is 15 to 30 seconds long.
- ☐ My commercial has a clear message about the benefits of vitamin D.
- ☐ I created the commercial to appeal to my target audience. (kids or adults)
- ☐ I practiced reading my commercial with expression.

"Sunlight and Vitamin D"—Think About It!

1. What are some things you can do to avoid sun damage to your skin?

____

____

____

2. You need one hour of sunlight each week. Fill in the chart below. Show how many minutes of sunlight you get (on average) each day.

	Mon.	Tues.	Wed.	Thurs.	Fri.	Sat.	Sun.
Amount of sunlight in minutes							

Total amount of sunlight in an average week: ________________ minutes.

If you did not get one hour of sunlight in a week, what could you do to get more?

____

____

3. List some advantages and disadvantages of spending more time outside in the sunlight.

Advantages	Disadvantages

Healthy Eating: Journal Topics

Eating a balanced diet is an important way of taking care of your body. Here are some questions to get you thinking about your eating habits.

1. Why do you think it is important to eat a balanced diet?
2. How do you think what you eat affects your body and the way you feel?
3. Do you think the media influences your eating habits? Explain your thinking.
4. What do you think the differences are between a snack and a treat?
5. Do your eating habits change? Do you eat differently when you are at home than when you are with your friends or out at a restaurant? Explain.
6. What can you do to maintain a healthy body weight?
7. Do you like to eat breakfast? Why or why not?
8. Are there any foods you refuse to eat? Explain.
9. Name some of your favorite foods. Why are they your favorite?
10. Do you check the nutritional information on the food items you eat? Why or why not?
11. Do you think convenience foods (frozen foods, canned foods, fast food) make it easier or more difficult to keep a healthy diet? Explain your thinking.

Fitness and Health

Your body is made of systems. These include your respiratory system and muscular system. They work together to help you do all the things you want to do. It is important to keep each of these systems healthy by staying fit. You can do this through regular exercise.

It Is Great to Be Fit

When you are fit, your heart can pump more efficiently. Your muscles are also stronger. You are more flexible and your joints move more easily. You do not get sick as often and your injuries heal faster. You also have improved balance. This makes you better at sports such as skiing, kayaking, and hockey.

Feel Good

Are you feeling stressed? Staying fit can help. People who exercise feel less stress. And exercising actually puts you in a better mood. When you work out, your brain releases chemicals that make you feel happier.

Zzzzzz

People who are fit sleep better. They fall asleep faster and they sleep more soundly.

Smoking

An easy way to help stay fit and healthy is to not smoke. Smoking damages your respiratory system. It also affects your whole body, since all of your systems are linked.

Every Day

You need about 60 minutes of exercise every day. That sounds like a lot, but you get exercise every time you walk up the stairs or walk to a friend's home. You also get exercise when you pick up a stack of books. Try to work all of your muscles every day by doing a variety of exercises.

Staying fit all your life will help you live longer and healthier.

"Fitness and Health"—Think About It!

1. List at least four ways to stay healthy.

2. Complete the web below on the benefits of staying fit.

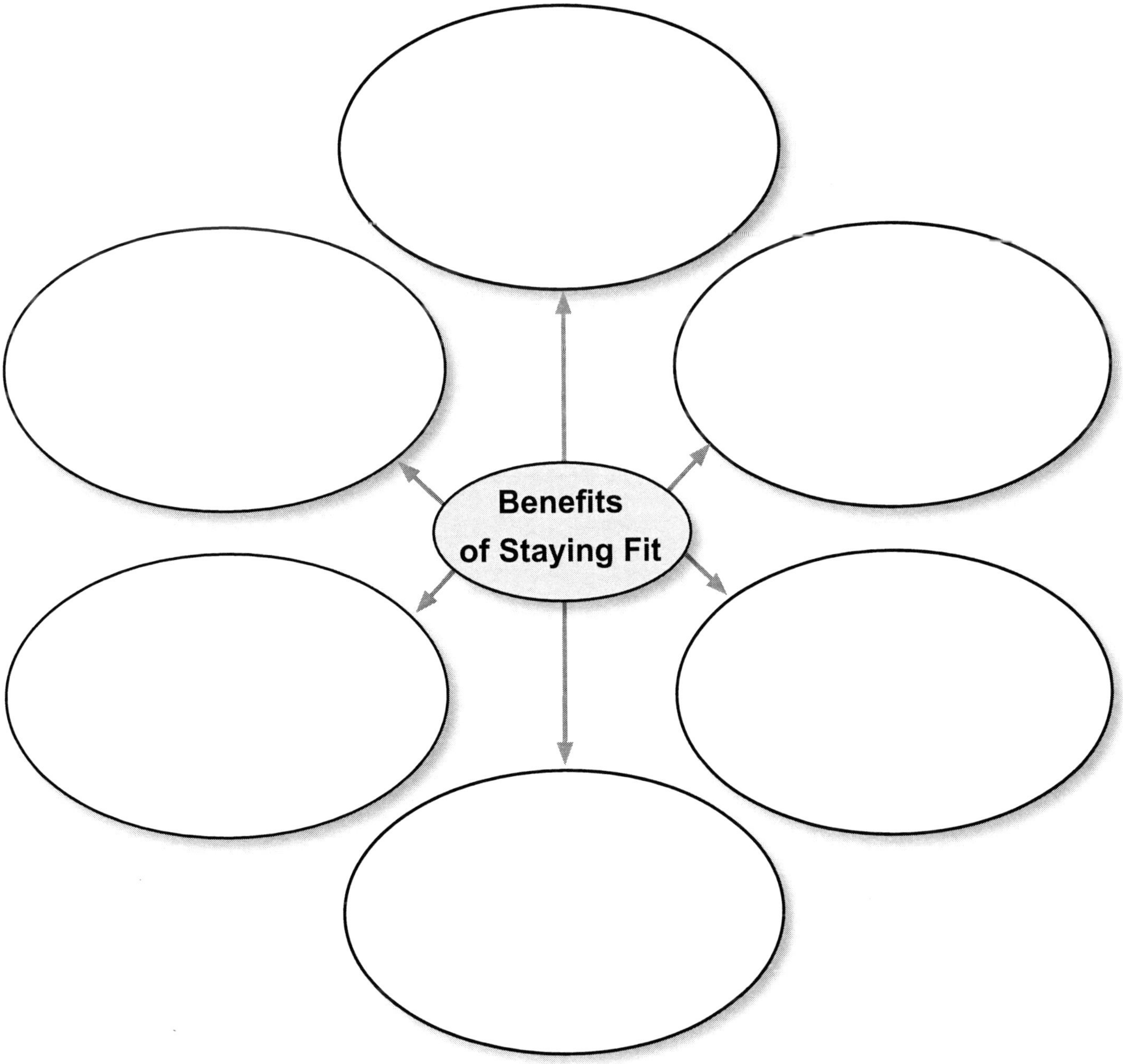

Create a Human Body Board Game

What You Need

- Scissors
- 2 number cubes
- Coloring materials
- Glue
- Construction paper
- A base for the game board, such as a large piece of bristol board, a clean pizza box, or a file folder

What You Do

1. Choose a base for the game board.
2. Create a path the game pieces will follow. You may choose to give your path a specific shape: a U shape, an L shape, a square, or an oval. Make your path at least 50 squares long.
3. Add spaces where you have to stack question cards cut from heavy paper. Print or handwrite questions on the cards. Print instructions on some game board spaces.
4. Test the game to see if it is too hard or has enough spaces.
5. Cut small figures out of paper to use as game pieces, or use materials that are available.
6. Decorate the game board to make it colorful so people know it is about the human body.
7. Write the rules and directions on how to play the game.

Rules and How to Play

- How does a player move around the board? Here are some ideas:
  - roll the number cubes
  - pick up a card and answer a question
  - follow the instructions on the game board spaces
- Are there penalties for wrong answers?
- How many people can play?

Ideas for Game Cards

Create questions about the human body to test players' knowledge. Create different categories such as

- true or false
- explain
- multiple choice

Ideas for Game Board Spaces

- miss a turn
- go back 5 spaces
- roll again

Two Basic Forces: Pushing and Pulling

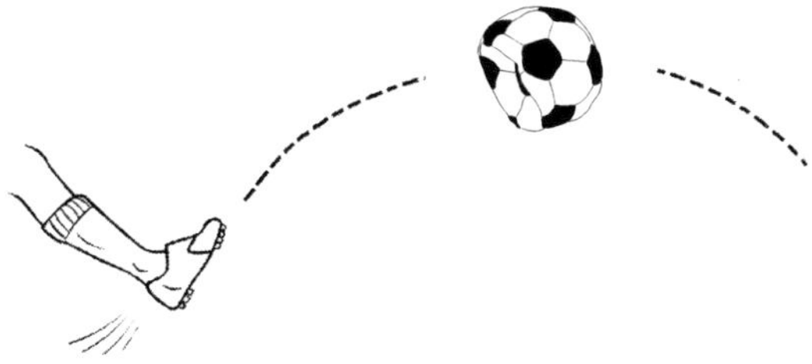

A force is something that can make an object change speed, shape, or direction. The forces of push and pull can do all three of these things. Here are some examples.

Pushing

- You are coasting along on a skateboard and you want to go faster. You use your foot to push backward on the sidewalk. This push gives you more speed.
- You have a wet ball of clay. You push down on it. The force of pushing changes the shape of the clay. It is no longer in the shape of a ball.
- A soccer ball is rolling toward you. You can push it in another direction.

Pulling

- You let go of a shopping cart on a hill, and it rolls away from you. You catch up with the cart and pull on it. By pulling, you change the speed of the shopping cart.
- You pull at each end to make an elastic band change its shape.
- You play with a yo-yo. You let go of the yo-yo to make it drop toward the ground. When it reaches the end of the string, you give it a quick upward pull. It changes direction and travels up, instead of down.

The Pulling Force of Gravity

Gravity is a force that pulls objects down toward Earth. When you let go of a ball, gravity is what makes it drop to Earth. Now, think about what happens when you throw a ball up in the air. Gravity slows down the speed of the ball until it stops traveling upward. Then gravity makes the ball start to travel down to the ground. The closer the ball gets to the ground, the faster it moves. This shows how the pulling force of gravity changes the speed and the direction of the ball.

Brain Stretch

What pushes and pulls can you see around you? How did you use forces today? Describe them on a separate piece of paper.

"Two Basic Forces: Pushing and Pulling"—Think About It!

1. Describe how you use the forces of pushing and pulling when you do the following activities.

a) Use a computer mouse: ______________________________

b) Brush your teeth: ______________________________

c) Ride a bicycle: ______________________________

2. Choose a sport (other than cycling) that you enjoy playing or watching. Explain how the forces of pushing and/or pulling are involved in playing the sport. If gravity plays a role, explain what it does.

3. When you blow up a balloon, your lungs push air into the balloon. Which does this pushing force cause a change in: speed, shape, or direction? Explain your answer.

Forces and Structures

What Is a Structure?

A structure is something that holds or supports a load. For example, a garden shed has four walls that support a roof.

Structures are built for one or more purposes. A garden shed provides a place to keep garden tools dry. A locked shed will also keep the tools safe so they will not be stolen.

What Types of Forces Act on Structures?

Two types of forces act on structures—internal forces and external forces.

Internal forces are part of the structure. For example, the roof of a house is heavy and pushes down on the outside walls. The roof is part of the structure of the house. If the walls are not strong enough to hold up the roof, the house will collapse. So the pushing force created by the weight of the roof is an internal force.

External forces come from things that are not part of the structure. For example, snow will push its weight down on the roof. The walls also have to be strong enough to support the weight of snow on the roof. Because the snow is not part of the structure, snow is an external force.

Two Types of Loads

Loads are forces that act on a structure. All structures need to be strong enough to hold up under the loads placed on them. Loads are divided into two categories—dead loads and live loads.

A **dead load** is a permanent load that does not leave. The weight of the materials used to build a structure are part of the dead load. Anything permanently attached to a structure is part of the dead load. Carpet and window planters are dead loads.

A **live load** is a load that is temporary. Objects that carry temporary loads are also part of the live load. Here are some examples:

- Furniture is part of the live load in a house. It can be removed from the house if you move to a new house.
- Snow that builds up on a house roof is a live load. Snow is temporary because it can melt away or be removed.

"Forces and Structures"—Think About It!

1. For each example below, identify whether it is a live or dead load. Explain your thinking.

a) Plumbing pipes

❑ live load ❑ dead load

Why I think so: ______________________________

____

____

b) An elevator in an office building

❑ live load ❑ dead load

Why I think so: ______________________________

____

____

c) The people who work in an office building

❑ live load ❑ dead load

Why I think so: ______________________________

____

____

d) Wind that blows against a structure on windy days

❑ live load ❑ dead load

Why I think so: ______________________________

____

____

e) The balconies in an apartment building

❑ live load ❑ dead load

Why I think so: ______________________________

____

____

Four Types of Internal Forces

An internal force is a force that acts from within the structure.
Let us look at four types of internal forces.

Imagine that we start with a rectangular block of material.

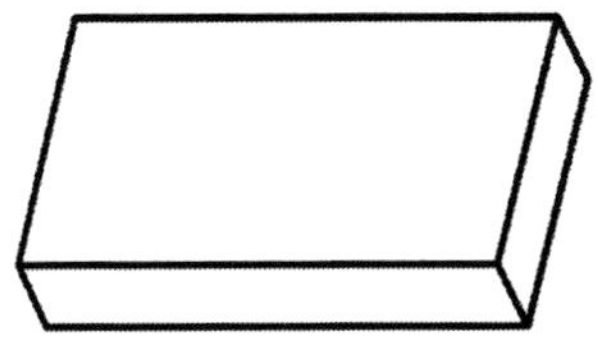

Compression is a pushing force that squeezes a material. This force often makes materials shorter.

Example: Hold a soft sponge flat in the palm of one hand. Push down on the top of the sponge with your other hand. You are creating compression.

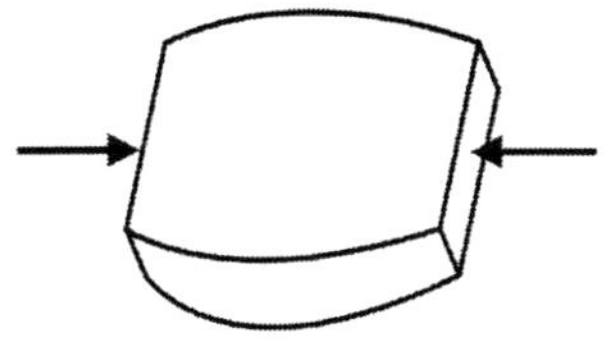

Tension is a pulling force that stretches a material. This force often makes materials longer.

Example: Hold one end of an elastic band in each hand. Move your hands farther apart. You are creating tension that stretches the elastic band.

Torsion is a twisting or turning force.

Example: To wring out a wet washcloth, you use the twisting force of torsion. You hold the washcloth in two hands and twist it to force out the water.

Bending is a force that makes a straight material curved. One side of the material squeezes together (compression). The other side stretches apart (tension).

Example: A soft or damp sponge is easy to bend. Hold it in both hands and bend it in the same way as shown in the diagram. Tension acts on the top side and compression acts on the bottom side.

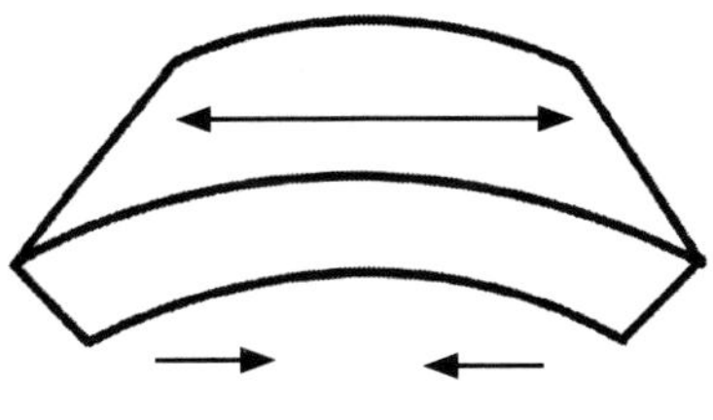

"Four Types of Internal Forces"—Think About It!

Identify the internal force at work in each of the examples below. Explain your thinking.

1. Ling loves sleeping on her new mattress. Her old mattress was as hard as a board. The new mattress sinks comfortably under her when she climbs into bed.

What type of internal force acts on the mattress when she lies on it? ____________________

____

____

2. Rick tunes his guitar. Rick tightens a guitar string to make it play in tune. To tighten it, he turns the tuning peg at the end of the guitar string.

a) What type of internal force acts on the guitar string? ____________________

____

____

b) What type of internal force acts on the tuning peg?

____

____

3. Maria and her brother Marco are making an autumn wreath for their door. The first step is to take a straight piece of wire and make it into a circle.

What type of internal force acts on the wire as they make it into a circle? ____________________

____

____

4. Mr. Green is fishing and a big fish has taken the bait. The fish tries to swim away as Mr. Green tries to reel it in.

What type of internal force acts on the fishing line? ____________________

____

____

____

Experimenting with Materials and Forces

How do different materials withstand internal forces? Try this experiment to find out.

What You Need

- Wooden craft stick
- Sponge
- Eraser
- Plastic straw
- New, unsharpened wooden pencil

What You Do

1. Read the rating scale at the bottom of this page.
2. Predict how well each material will withstand each force. Use the rating scale to make your predictions. Record your predictions in the results chart on the next page.
3. Test how well each material withstands tension. Pull on each material from both ends. Use the rating scale for each material and record the results in the chart.
4. Test how well each material withstands compression. Push on each material from both ends. Use the rating scale for each material and record the results in the chart.
5. Test how well each material withstands torsion. Twist each end in a different direction. Use the rating scale for each material and record the results in the chart.
6. Test how well each material withstands bending. Press down on each end with your fingers. Press up in the middle with your thumbs. (Do not waste classroom materials! See if the pencil will bend without using enough force to break it.) Use the rating scale for each material and record the results in the chart.

Rating Scale	
1	**Weak:** A very small amount of force makes the material change shape or break.
2	**Fair:** A small amount of force makes the material change shape or break.
3	**Good:** A lot of force makes the material change shape or break.
4	**Very Strong:** A lot of force makes no change or very little change in the material's shape.

"Experimenting with Materials and Forces"—Think About It!

Use the chart below and the rating scale on page 29 to record your predictions and results.

Material	Tension	Compression	Torsion	Bending
Wooden craft stick	Prediction: ______ Result: ______	Prediction: ______ Result: ______	Prediction: ______ Result: ______	Prediction: ______ Result: ______
Sponge	Prediction: ______ Result: ______	Prediction: ______ Result: ______	Prediction: ______ Result: ______	Prediction: ______ Result: ______
Eraser	Prediction: ______ Result: ______	Prediction: ______ Result: ______	Prediction: ______ Result: ______	Prediction: ______ Result: ______
Plastic straw	Prediction: ______ Result: ______	Prediction: ______ Result: ______	Prediction: ______ Result: ______	Prediction: ______ Result: ______
Pencil	Prediction: ______ Result: ______	Prediction: ______ Result: ______	Prediction: ______ Result: ______	Prediction: ______ Result: ______

Below, record any notes about your results or any questions you wonder about.

Forces and Shapes

Strong shapes are used when people design buildings. These shapes make buildings that can withstand the forces that act on them. Three strong shapes are often used in buildings. These shapes are rectangles, arches, and triangles.

In the diagrams below, the pairs of arrows show the following forces at work:

← → tension   → ← compression

Rectangles

A rectangle can be quite strong. But it is not as strong when a force pushes on one of the vertical sides. Its shape can change, making it weaker. Builders add a diagonal support piece to make the rectangle stronger. This support piece is called a brace. It goes between two opposite corners of the rectangle.

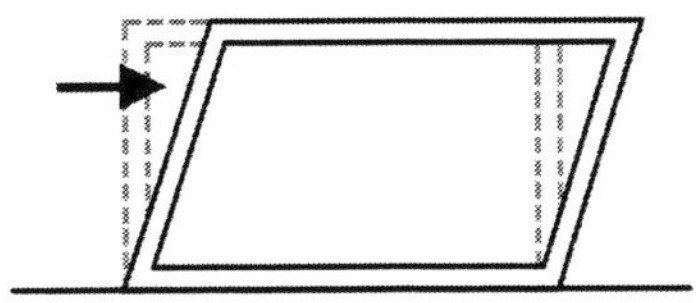

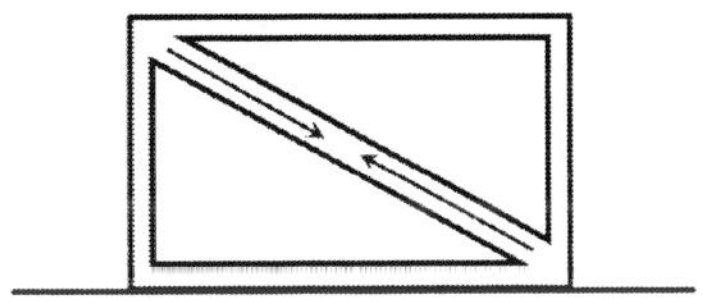

Arches

An arch is a strong shape. But it is not as strong when a force pushes down on the top of the arch. When a force pushes down on it, the sides of the arch spread outward. To make an arch stronger, builders add supports on each side. These supports are called buttresses. The buttresses prevent the sides of the arch from spreading outward.

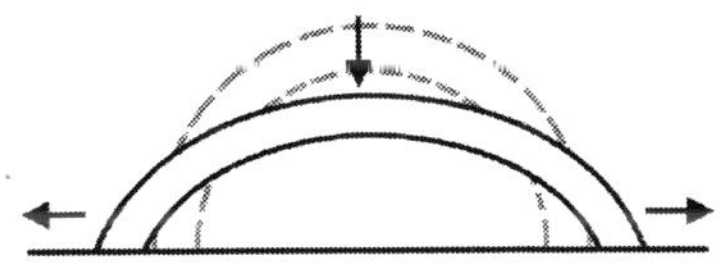

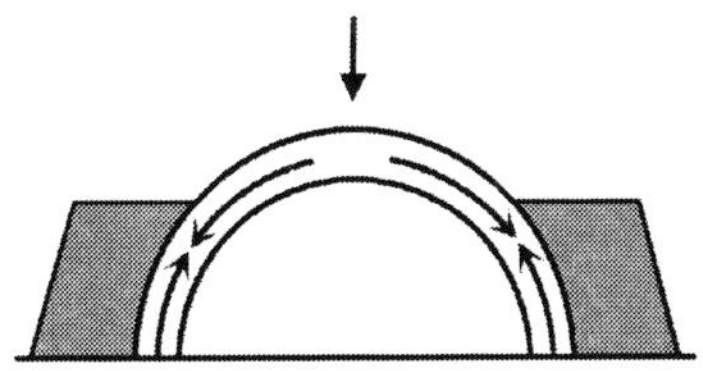

Triangles

A triangle can be a very strong shape. If a force pushes on the top point, the triangle is very strong. But if a force pushes on the side of a triangle, the side can bend.

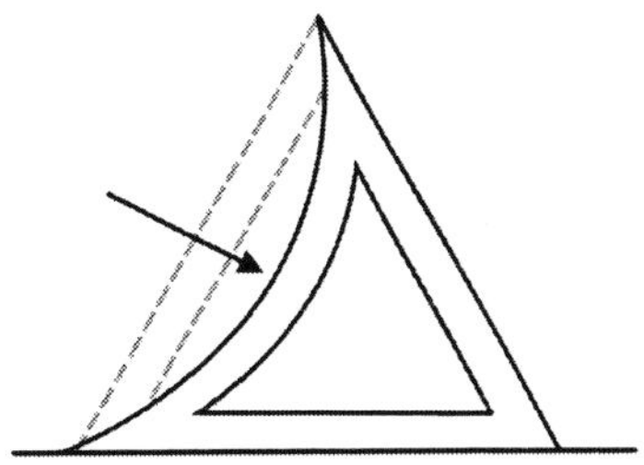

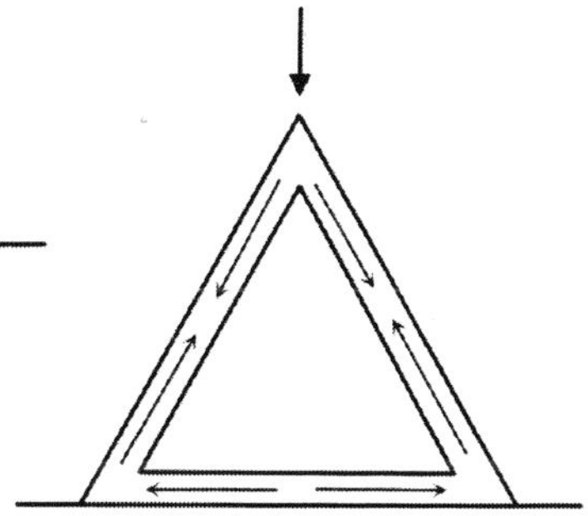

"Forces and Shapes"—Think About It!

1. A pushing force is applied to the side of a rectangle. What internal force acts on the brace?

____

2. A force pushes down on the top point of a triangle.

a) What internal force acts on the two sloping sides of a triangle?

____

b) What internal force acts on the bottom of the triangle?

____

3. Some houses have a sloped roof that forms a triangle. The top point of the triangle does not support any weight. But the sloping sides are useful in areas where it rains and snows.

a) What might happen to a flat roof if a storm brings a lot of snow? Why?

____

____

b) Which roof would be safer for a house built in an area that gets a lot of snow: a triangular roof or a flat roof? Why?

____

____

c) A triangular roof is not easily damaged by rain. Why?

____

____

4. a) What two shapes are used to build an igloo?

____

b) You have built an igloo and you know that a heavy snowfall is coming. How could you make the igloo's entrance strong enough to support the weight of the snow? (Snow is the only material you have to work with.)

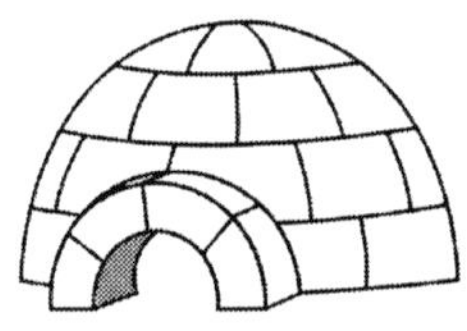

____

____

Four Types of Bridges

In the diagrams below, the pairs of arrows show the following forces at work:

← → tension   → ← compression

Beam Bridge

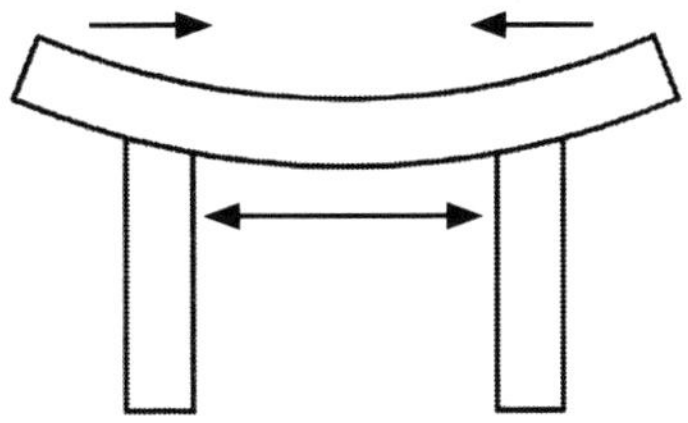

A beam bridge has a horizontal beam supported by two piers. The beam bends when a load is on the bridge. A load can be cars, trucks, or a train. Compression acts on the top side of the beam. Tension acts on the bottom side of the beam.

Arch Bridge

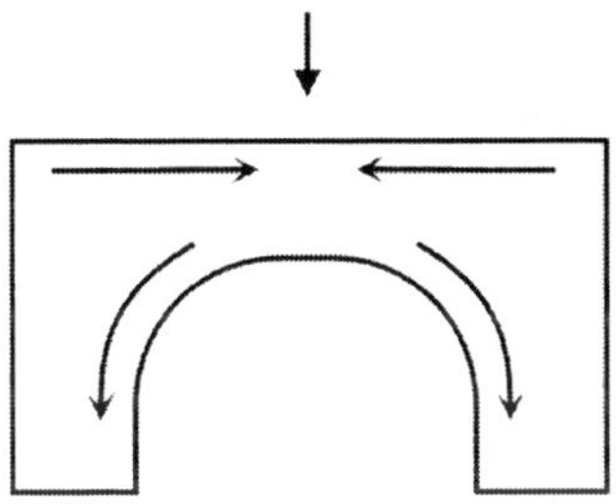

The arch is a very strong shape. A load on top of the bridge causes compression on the top of the bridge. It also causes tension along the arch underneath the bridge. This tension could cause the arch to spread apart, making it weaker. The material on the sides of the arch acts like buttresses. It keeps the arch from spreading apart.

Truss Bridge

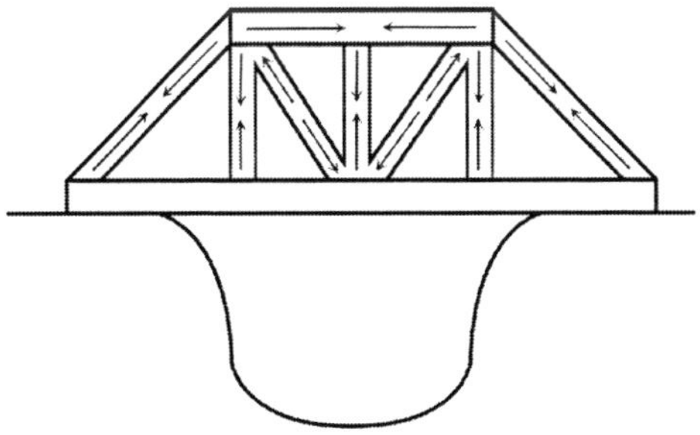

A truss bridge is built with triangles made of steel bars. A triangle is a very strong shape. Compression and tension forces act on the bridge. The diagram below shows the forces.

Suspension Bridge

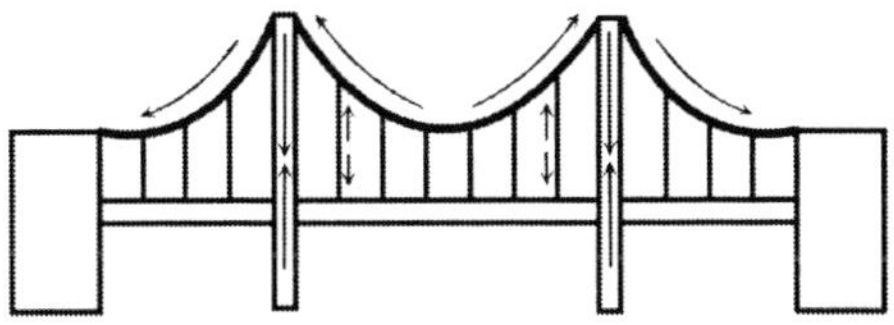

On a suspension bridge, tall towers support the main cable. Smaller cables attached to the main cable support the roadway. These cables are called suspenders. The main cable is attached to large blocks at each end of the bridge. The load of traffic on the bridge is transferred to the suspenders. This causes tension in the suspenders. The suspenders transfer the load to the main cable. This causes tension in the cables. Compression acts on the towers as they support the weight of the bridge and the traffic.

"Four Types of Bridges"—Think About It!

1. Snow and ice can build up on the roadway of a bridge, making it heavier. Are snow and ice internal or external forces? Explain your answer.

2. A simple beam bridge can be built over a stream. All you need are two blocks and a wooden plank.

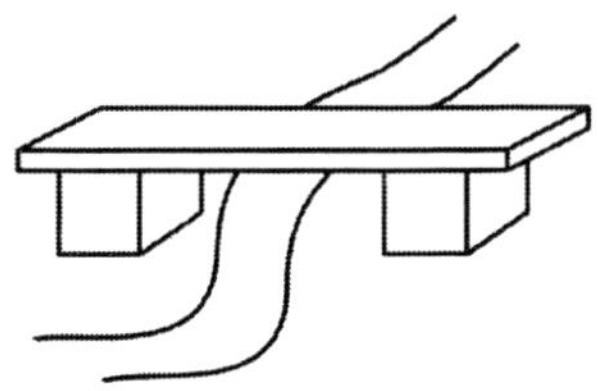

a) What force acts on the blocks when someone is crossing the bridge?

b) What force (or forces) will act on the plank?

c) Is the weight of the plank an internal or external force?

3. You are designing a bridge that will take tour buses to an interesting place. Explain why you would need to know the following information:

a) The maximum number of people that can fit in one bus

b) The maximum number of buses that can fit on the bridge

Plastic Straw Bridge Challenge

Build a bridge out of straws that holds as much weight as possible.

What You Need

- Plastic straws
- Masking tape
- Scissors
- 100 pennies in a plastic cup
- 2 desks of equal height

What You Do

1. Sketch out a design of a bridge before building it.
2. You can only use scissors to cut the straws.
3. You can only use masking tape to hold the bridge together.
4. The bridge should span two desks 3 ft (100 cm) apart.
5. Once complete, test the bridge by seeing how many pennies it can hold.

Think About It!

1. Sketch a drawing of your bridge on a separate piece of paper.

2. Predict how many pennies you think your bridge will hold. ____________________

3. What happened when you added pennies to test your bridge?

____

____

____

4. How many pennies can your bridge hold? ____________________

5. What are some ways to improve your design?

____

____

____

Try this challenge using another material such as spaghetti!

Watch Out for Wind!

Nature's Forces

Some of the external forces that affect structures come from nature. When snow and ice build up on a structure, they add weight. The structure must be able to support that weight. An earthquake is an external force that occurs when large sections of Earth's crust start to move. These sections are called tectonic plates. This movement causes the ground to shake. The shaking can make structures such as buildings collapse.

Hurricanes and Tornadoes

Wind is another of nature's forces. Strong winds push against structures. The force of the wind can damage or destroy structures such as homes. Tornadoes and hurricanes have very strong winds. These winds can cause severe damage. Some people live in areas where these storms often happen. They must find ways to make their homes withstand the force of strong wind.

Protecting Structures from Wind

Strong wind can push against windows, causing them to shatter. Some people nail pieces of plywood over the windows to protect them.

A very strong wind can have enough force to lift the roof off a house. The structure of the house is much weaker once the roof is gone. The house may collapse. Some people use hurricane ties to attach the roof more securely to the house. Hurricane ties are strips of steel. They can withstand much more force than the nails that join the roof to the house.

Because of the threat of hurricanes or tornados, some buildings are made from different materials. They are not made from wood or bricks. Instead, they are built from reinforced concrete. Reinforced concrete has steel bars running through it. This material can withstand very strong winds.

Wind Makes Waves

Hurricanes form over oceans and they sometimes move over land. Hurricane winds can cause large waves. These waves can damage houses built along the ocean shore. One way to protect a house from wave damage is to build it above the ground. Steel, concrete, or wood is used to create pillars. These pillars are called pilings. The house is built on top of the pilings so waves can travel under the house without damaging it.

"Watch Out for Wind!"—Think About It!

1. When strong winds become dangerous, people often seek shelter in a basement. Why is a basement a good place to go?

2. During a hurricane or tornado, people are told to go to a safe place in their home. They are also told to cover themselves with a heavy blanket. Why might they use a blanket?

3. A special type of nail can be used for building homes. One feature of this nail is that it has rings that create sharp points. (See the cross-section diagram.) Would this nail help wooden structures to survive a hurricane or tornado? Why?

4. People look for new ideas for creating safer homes in hurricane areas. One idea is to make houses in the shape of a dome. Would a house built in this shape be less likely to be damaged in a hurricane? Why?

Protect Yourself!

Playing sports can be lots of fun, and the exercise is very good for you. But playing sports can also cause injuries. It is important to protect yourself with the proper safety equipment.

Forces and Sports

In many sports, things move fast. The players, as well as things such as balls and pucks, all move fast. In baseball, the pitcher throws the ball at a high speed. A ball moving at high speed it is harder to hit. The pitcher's throw is a pushing force. That force sends the ball speeding toward the batter. The batter uses a pushing force to swing the bat. When the bat hits the ball, it changes the direction of the ball. The bat sends the ball sailing into the outfield. A ball that is moving quickly has a large amount of force. When the ball comes in contact with a person, the force is transferred to the person's body. Without safety equipment, this force can cause serious injuries.

Players also move quickly in many sports. The players use their legs to create a pushing force that moves them forward. In some sports, players can move *really* fast. A hockey player can race down the ice faster than a person can run. A person riding a skateboard can move extremely fast when going down a hill. (This is because of wheels and the force of gravity.) If a fast-moving player falls or crashes into something, they can be injured.

Sports Safety Equipment

Most sports safety equipment protects players in three ways:

- **Absorbing force:** Many types of safety equipment have foam padding. This absorbs some of the force of a speeding ball or puck. It can even protect them from another player. Less of the force is transferred to the player's body. This means there is less chance of a player being injured.

- **Spreading out force:** A puck moves very fast. If it hits you in the head, the force of the puck is transferred to your head. So a lot of force is transferred to the small part of your head the puck hits. A helmet will spread the puck's force over a larger area. This makes the force less intense in any one spot. This means you are less likely to be injured by the force. The foam padding inside a helmet will also absorb some of the force.
- **Protecting skin:** Scrapes and cuts are usually not serious injuries. But they can hurt and might become infected if not looked after properly. Safety equipment protects skin. An example is hockey skates made from thick leather. They are made to support and protect a player's feet and ankles. They also protect them from being cut by another player's skate blade.

"Protect Yourself!"—Think About It!

1. Hockey goalies wear thick leg pads. Other players do not wear the same type of leg pads. Why do goalies need extra protection for their legs?

2. a) How do the cushioned soles of running shoes protect runners?

   b) Cushioned soles need to be able to withstand two internal forces: compression and bending. Explain why.

3. The foam padding inside a helmet is like a sponge. It can absorb the force of compression by becoming thinner. It is very important not to wear a helmet that fits too tightly. Explain why.

4. Skateboarders should crouch down on the skateboard if they are about to fall. Why? How would this help to protect skateboarders?

Structures and the Environment

Humans build many types of structures. They build office towers and shopping malls. They also build bridges, and steel towers that support electrical lines. All of these structures affect the environment.

Negative Effects of Structures

Building a structure can damage the environment. Here are some examples:

- Natural environments can be destroyed when the land is prepared for construction. These environments provide habitats for plants and animals.
- Building materials have to be brought to the site, sometimes from places far away. The trucks that bring the materials pollute the air. They also cause noise pollution.
- The materials used in construction can damage the environment. For example, steel is made from iron, which comes from mines. The stone used to create concrete comes from quarries. Mines and quarries damage the beauty of natural environments and create pollution.
- Materials such as iron and stone are turned into steel and concrete in large factories. These factories use a lot of energy and create pollution.

Positive Effects of Structures

Some of the structures people build have a positive effect on the environment.

- Bridges and boardwalks help protect fragile environments, such as marshes and sand dunes, that would be damaged by visitors' footsteps.
- Wind generators are giant windmills. They produce electricity from the force of the wind. Wind generators make little pollution. That is why they are sometimes called a source of "clean energy" or "green energy."
- What grows on a solar farm? Nothing! Solar farms are large areas covered with large structures called solar panels. These structures turn sunlight into electricity. They do not put any pollution into the air.
- Tunnels under roads let animals travel safely to other areas of their habitat without being hit by a car.

"Structures and the Environment"—Think About It!

1. Wind generators and bridges have positive effects on the environment. But it is impossible to create these structures without damaging the environment. List two ways in which creating these structures damage the environment.

2. Tina found out that a bridge will be built across the river near her town. She wonders if having a ferry take cars across the river would be better. A ferry would have these advantages for the environment:

- Less construction equipment would be required at the site. This equipment can damage the natural landscape.
- Producing the steel and concrete needed for the bridge will damage the environment. A ferry requires less material.

List two ways in which a ferry could have negative effects on the environment.

3. Tina's community holds a town hall meeting. They discuss whether a bridge or a ferry is the better solution. Which option do you think each of the following groups would choose? Explain why.

a) Unemployed construction workers

b) People who like to fish in the part of the river where the ferry would operate

Forces and Structures Quiz

Test your knowledge of forces and structures by answering the questions below.

1. A force can make an object change ____________________, ______________________, or

________________________.

2. A ball is thrown straight up in the air. How does gravity affect its speed and direction?

____

____

3. Describe the difference between an external force and an internal force.

____

____

____

4. Name each of the forces described below.

a) A twisting or turning force: __________________________

b) A force that makes a straight material become curved: __________________________

c) A pulling forces that stretches a material: __________________________

d) A pushing force that squeezes a material: __________________________

5. Draw two shapes that make structures stronger.

6. Sports safety equipment helps protect players from injury. List three types of protection equipment gives.

____

____

____

What Is Matter?

Everything you see around you is made of matter. Matter is anything that has mass and takes up space.

Mass and Volume

Mass is the amount of matter in an object. Matter is made up of tiny particles. Since every object is made of particles, every object has mass. The more particles an object has, the greater its mass is.

Volume is the amount of space that matter takes up. It is easy to see that different objects take up different amounts of space. A baseball takes up more space than a marble, so a baseball has greater volume than a marble.

Comparing Mass and Volume

If two objects have the same volume, do they have the same mass? Not necessarily. Remember that objects are made of matter, and matter is made of particles. Two objects that are the same size can be made up of different numbers of particles. Why? In some materials, the particles are packed more tightly together.

Imagine you have two solid blocks, one made of wood and one of steel. The blocks are exactly the same size, so they have the same volume. Do they have the same mass? No. The particles in steel are packed together more tightly than the particles in wood. So there are more particles in the steel block than in the wooden block. As you can probably guess, the block of steel would weigh more than the block of wood.

In the same way, two objects with the same mass might not have the same volume. One pound (kilogram) of wool takes up a lot more space than one pound (kilogram) of marbles. They have the same mass. But the particles in wool are more spread out.

Brain Stretch

Mass is measured on a scale. It measures the pull of gravity on your mass. If you travel to the Moon, your mass will not change. But a scale on the Moon will say you weigh less. The Moon's gravity does not pull as much as Earth's gravity.

"What Is Matter?"—Think About It!

1. Which of the following are made of matter? Put a check mark in the appropriate box.

a) Elephant	❑ Matter	❑ Not matter
b) Ping-pong ball	❑ Matter	❑ Not matter
c) Window glass	❑ Matter	❑ Not matter
d) Maple syrup	❑ Matter	❑ Not matter
e) Hair	❑ Matter	❑ Not matter
f) Fog	❑ Matter	❑ Not matter

2. You have two cubes, each made of a different material. One cube is slightly larger than the other.

a) Circle the sentence that has to be true.

A. The larger cube has more mass than the smaller cube.

B. The smaller cube has less volume than the larger cube.

b) Explain why two objects that have the same volume might not have the same mass.

____

____

____

3. For each pair of objects, put a check mark beside the object that has the greater volume.

a) ❑ a grapefruit ❑ a watermelon b) ❑ a dime ❑ a quarter

4. Salima is doing an experiment to compare two objects. First, she fills two identical glasses with the same amount of water. When she drops the first object into a glass, the water level rises but the water does not overflow. When she drops the second object into the other glass, the water overflows.

a) Which property of matter is Salima investigating: mass, volume, or both? ________________

b) Complete the sentence to tell what Salima learned about the objects.

The second object has ____________________________________ than the first object.

Properties of Matter

What Are Properties?

Objects have different properties. Properties are characteristics that we can notice with our five senses, or characteristics that we can measure or test.

Types of Properties

You can easily tell the difference between a lemon and a lime because your sense of sight tells you that one is yellow and the other is green. Color is a property. Mass and volume are two other properties of matter. You can measure these properties.

Solubility—how easily a substance dissolves in a liquid. If you put sand in a glass of water and stir, the sand will not dissolve. It is not soluble. If you put sugar in a glass of water and stir, the sugar will dissolve. Sugar is soluble. Some substances dissolve more easily than others.

Viscosity—how easily a substance flows. Imagine pouring a cup of milk and a cup of honey. Which will pour out first? The milk, of course! Viscosity is really about how much a substance *resists* flowing. Honey has higher viscosity than milk because honey resists flowing more than milk does.

Transparency—how well light passes through a substance. If the substance is clear (you can see objects through it), it is *transparent.* If light passes through the substance, but you cannot see objects through it, it is *translucent.* If no light passes through the substance, it is *opaque.*

Hardness—how easily an object changes shape. A hard object, such as a rock, does not change shape easily. A soft object, such as a pillow, changes shape easily. If you push down on a pillow—even with very little force—you will make a dent in it. The shape of the pillow has changed.

Why is it important to understand the properties of matter? People who design products consider the properties of the materials they use. For example, if you are going to make sponges or diapers, you will need to consider the absorbency of the materials you use. Materials and the products we make from them are all made of matter.

sponge

"Properties of Matter"—Think About It!

1. Bath towels and dish towels are usually made of cotton. Use two of the properties mentioned on the previous page to explain why cotton is a good material to use for towels.

2. It can take a while for ketchup to flow out of the bottle.

   a) Does this mean that ketchup has a high viscosity, or a low viscosity?

   b) Give three other properties of ketchup.

3. The plastic wraps that we use to keep food fresh are transparent. Why is the property of transparency useful in a plastic wrap?

4. Jim is inventing a new type of powdered drink that can be mixed with water. When he tested it out by mixing it in a glass of water, he found that the powder has low solubility. What did Jim see when he looked in the glass after adding the powder and stirring it?

5. Give four properties of your desk.

Experiment: Do All Liquids Dissolve in Water?

When people wash dishes by hand, they use a liquid dish detergent. The dish detergent does not sit in a glob in the bottom of the sink—it dissolves in the water. Try this experiment to see if all liquids dissolve in water.

What You Need

- Isopropyl alcohol (rubbing alcohol)
- Corn syrup
- Vegetable oil
- Water
- 6 clear plastic cups
- Masking tape
- Straw
- 1 tsp (5 mL) measure
- 1 tbsp (15 mL) measure

SAFETY ALERT

Do **not** drink any of the liquids in this experiment.

What You Do

1. Use pieces of masking tape to label three of the cups with these labels: Alcohol, Corn Syrup, Vegetable Oil.
2. Use masking tape to create labels for the other three cups: Alcohol + Water, Corn Syrup + Water, Vegetable Oil + Water.
3. Pour 2 tsp (10 mL) of alcohol into the cup with the appropriate label. (Use the cup with the label "Alcohol," **not** the cup labeled "Alcohol + Water.")
4. Pour 2 tsp (10 mL) of corn syrup into the appropriate cup, and 2 tsp (10 mL) of vegetable oil into the appropriate cup.
5. Pour 2 tbsp (30 mL) of water into each of the cups with "+ Water" on the label.
6. Pour the alcohol into the cup labeled "Alcohol + Water." Observe the cup from the side as you pour. Watch what happens and record your observations on the next page.

7. Stir the alcohol and water and see whether the alcohol seems to dissolve in the water. (Keep watching from the side.) Record your observations.
8. Repeat steps 6 and 7 for each of the other two liquids (corn syrup and vegetable oil). Make sure you pour each liquid into the correct cup. Record your observations after doing each step.

"Experiment: Do All Liquids Dissolve in Water?"—Think About It!

1. What did you observe when you poured alcohol into the water?

2. What did you observe when you stirred the alcohol and water?

3. What did you observe when you poured the corn syrup into the water?

4. What did you observe when you stirred the corn syrup and water?

5. What did you observe when you poured the vegetable oil into the water?

6. What did you observe when you stirred the vegetable oil and water?

7. What is your conclusion—do all liquids dissolve in water?

States of Matter

Anything that has mass and takes up space is matter. Matter can exist in three different states—solid, liquid, or gas. Each of these states has different properties.

Solids

A solid holds its shape. For example, a rock is a solid. If you put a rock in a box, the rock will not take on the shape of the box.

Solids have a definite volume. The volume of a solid does not change. (Remember that volume is the amount of space that matter takes up.) A solid always takes up the same amount of space.

Liquids

Liquids take on the shape of the container they are in. For example, a fishbowl and an aquarium have different shapes. When you pour water into each container, the water takes on the shape of the container.

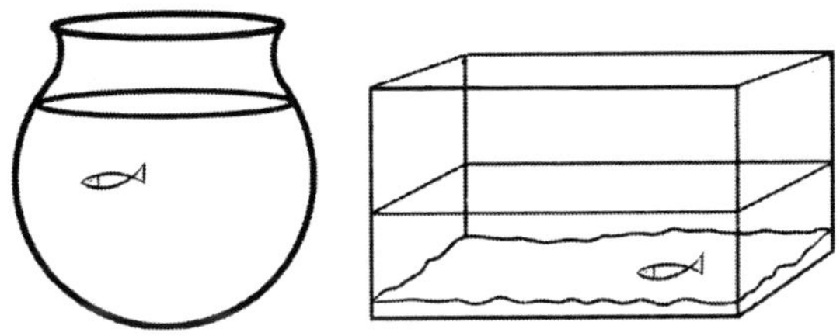

Liquids have a definite volume. Even though the shape of a liquid can change, it always takes up the same amount of space. Imagine that you fill a fishbowl with water. Then, you pour the water into an aquarium. The shape of the water changes, but its volume does not.

Gases

Most gases are invisible. We cannot see the air we breathe, but air is made up of different gases. When wind blows, we can feel these gases moving against our skin. Steam from a boiling kettle is a gas.

Gases do not have a definite shape. They take on the shape of the container they are in.

Gases do not have a definite volume. If you put a small amount of gas into a large container, the gas will spread out to fill the container.

Comparing Properties of Solids, Liquids, and Gases

State	Shape	Volume
Solid	- holds its shape	- has a definite volume
Liquid	- takes on the shape of its container	- has a definite volume
Gas	- takes on the shape of its container	- does not have a definite volume

"States of Matter"—Think About It!

1. Put each of the following in the correct column of the chart.

- **a drop of water**
- **oxygen in the air**
- **a pencil**
- **an elastic band**
- **ink in a marker**
- **steam from hot soup**
- **flowing lava**

Solid	Liquid	Gas

2. While watching a science show on television, Jenny heard about a substance that expands to take up more space without changing from one state to another.

   Beside statements a) to c) write "True" or "False."

   a) The substance has a definite volume. ____________________

   b) The substance cannot be an example of matter. ____________________

   c) The substance could be either a liquid or a gas. ____________________

   d) Is the substance that Jenny heard about a gas, liquid, or solid? How do you know?

   ____

   ____

   ____

   ____

3. Rick gets on an empty elevator and smells perfume. When he crouches down low, the scent is just as strong as when he is standing.

   a) What is Rick smelling: a solid, liquid, or gas? ____________________

   b) Why is the scent just as strong when Rick is standing or crouching?

   ____

   ____

   ____

Experiment: What State Is It In?

Shaving foam is made of soap, but it is not hard like a bar of soap or runny like liquid soap. Can we classify shaving foam as a solid, liquid, or gas? Try the experiment below.

What You Need

- Paper towel
- Shaving foam (not shaving gel)
- Penny
- Magnifying glass
- Ruler

What You Do

1. Place a blob of shaving foam on a piece of paper towel. Your blob of shaving foam should be roughly circular, 1.5 to 2 in (4 to 5 cm) in diameter, and about 1 in (3 cm) high. Observe the shaving foam for a moment, then answer question 1.
2. Very gently lay a penny flat on top of the shaving foam. Observe what happens and answer question 2. Then carefully remove the penny.
3. Look at the shaving foam through a magnifying glass. Answer question 3.
4. Using your index finger, scoop up a little of the shaving foam. Rub it between your thumb and fingers and notice how it feels. Answer question 4.
5. Put the blob of shaving foam in a place where it will not be disturbed. Leave it for two or three days. Then observe any changes in how it looks and feels, and answer questions 5 and 6.

Think About It!

1. A solid keeps its shape when it is not in a container.
   a) Does the blob of shaving foam keep its shape? ___________________
   b) Would you say that shaving foam is a solid? Why or why not?

   ____

   ____

   ____

2. a) What happened when you put the penny on top of the shaving foam?

   ____

   ____

"Experiment: What State Is It In?"—Think About It!

b) Would you now say the shaving foam is a solid, liquid, or gas? Why?

____

____

____

3. a) What did you observe when you looked at the shaving foam through a magnifying glass?

____

____

b) Based on what you saw, would you say that shaving foam is a solid, liquid, or gas?

____

____

4. a) How does the shaving foam feel when you rub it between your fingers?

____

____

b) Based on how the shaving foam feels on your fingers, what state would you say it is: a solid, liquid, or gas? ______________________________

5. a) What changes do you notice after leaving the shaving foam for two or three days?

____

____

b) Based on what you observe, what state would you say the shaving foam is now: a solid, liquid, or gas Why?

____

____

____

6. Based on all your observations, what is shaving foam: a solid, a liquid, a gas, or something else? Explain your thinking.

____

____

____

Changes in States of Matter

Matter can change from one state to another. For example, we can freeze a liquid to turn it into a solid. We can melt a solid to turn it into a liquid. We can boil a liquid to turn it into a gas. When matter changes state, heat is involved.

From Solid to Liquid: Melting

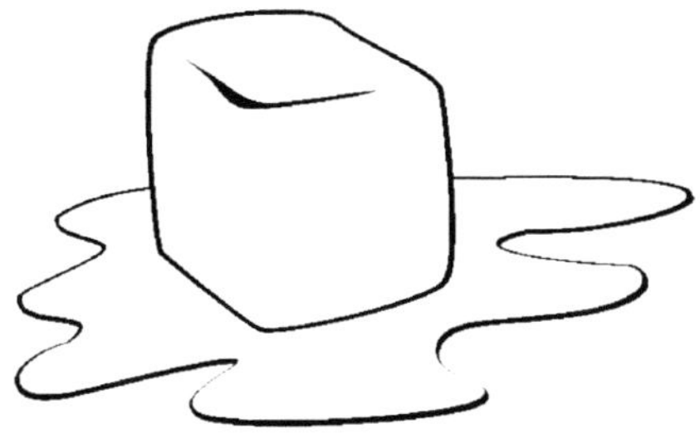

Melting is a process that changes a solid into a liquid. Solids melt when they absorb heat. An icicle melts when it absorbs heat from the air around it. An ice cube melts in a glass of water, even when the water is cold. Why? Cold water is warmer than an ice cube, so the ice cube can absorb heat from the water.

From Liquid to Gas: Evaporation

Evaporation is the process that changes a liquid into a gas. Liquids evaporate when they absorb heat. Steam coming out of a boiling kettle is water that has turned into a gas by evaporating.

From Gas to Liquid: Condensation

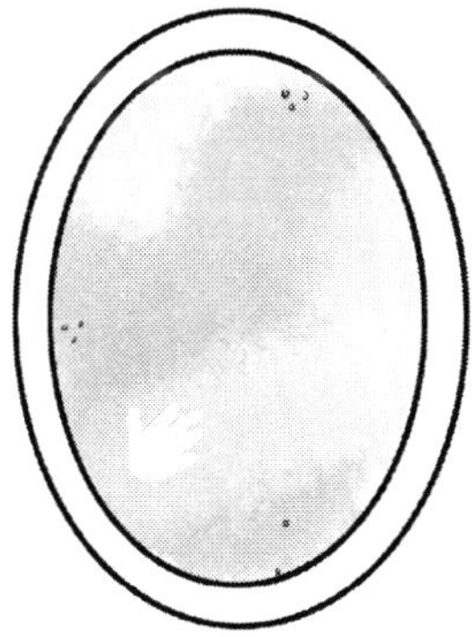

Condensation is the process that turns a gas into a liquid. Gases condense when they release heat. When you get out of a hot shower, the mirror in your bathroom may look misty or cloudy. This is caused by condensation. Some of the hot water from the shower evaporates, becoming water vapor (steam) in the air. The water vapor releases heat when it touches the mirror, which is cooler than the vapor. The vapor condenses into the tiny drops of water that cloud your mirror.

From Liquid to Solid: Freezing

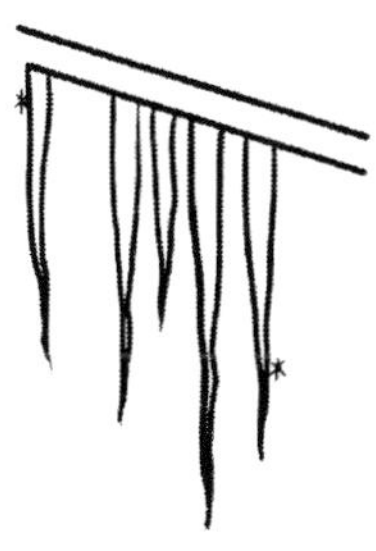

Freezing is the process that changes a liquid into a solid. Water freezes when the air around it is cold enough. The cold air makes the water release heat. Why can you not make ice cubes in a refrigerator? The air in a refrigerator is not cold enough to make the water release enough heat to turn into ice. (The process of changing from a liquid to a solid is sometimes called *solidification*.)

From Solid to Gas: Sublimation

Sublimation is the process that changes a solid into a gas. This change of state happens when the solid absorbs heat. Mothballs are small white balls with a strong odour that keeps moths away. (Moths like to eat certain types of material.) Over time, mothballs get smaller and smaller. That happens because mothballs contain chemicals that sublimate. The mothball does not change into a liquid before becoming a gas.

You can change ice into a gas by first melting the ice, then heating the water until it evaporates. This is *not* an example of sublimation because you first changed the solid (ice) into a liquid (water) before changing it into a gas (water vapor). In sublimation, a solid changes into a gas without first becoming a liquid.

From Gas to Solid: Deposition

Deposition is the process that changes a gas into a solid. This change of state happens when gas releases heat. Snowflakes are formed through deposition. When the air is cold enough, water vapor (a gas) in the air changes directly into ice (a solid) without becoming a liquid first. Deposition also creates the frost that forms on plants. When a leaf is cold enough, water vapor in the air changes state to become the ice we see on the leaf.

"Changes in States of Matter"—Think About It!

1. Complete as much as you can of the charts below without looking back at the article. Then review the article to find any information missing from your charts, and to correct any incorrect information.

	Changing from a...	**Into a...**	**The process is called...**
a)			Condensation
b)		Liquid	
c)	Solid		Sublimation
d)	Gas	Solid	
e)	Liquid	Gas	
f)			Freezing

	To change from a...	**Into a...**	**Is heat absorbed or released?**
g)	Solid	Liquid	
h)	Solid	Gas	
i)	Liquid	Solid	
j)	Gas	Liquid	
k)	Liquid	Gas	
l)	Gas	Solid	

2. For each process below, name the opposite process. For example, melting (changing a solid into a liquid) is the opposite of freezing (changing a liquid into a solid).

a) Condensation ______________________________

b) Sublimation ______________________________

c) Melting ______________________________

Physical Changes and Chemical Changes

Changes in matter can be physical changes or chemical changes. Physical changes are reversible, and chemical changes are irreversible (cannot be reversed).

Physical Changes

Changes in states of matter are always physical changes because they can be reversed. For example, you can melt an ice cube (a solid), then freeze the water (a liquid) to turn it back into ice. Or, you can boil water to make it evaporate into water vapor (a gas), then cool the water vapor to make it condense into liquid water. In both examples, the substance—water—has not changed into something else. The water changes from one state to another, but it is still always water.

Changes in states of matter are not the only types of physical change. If you cut an apple into two pieces, you have changed the shape of the apple but both pieces are still apple. You can reverse the change by putting the two pieces back together.

Chemical Changes

In a chemical change, a new substance—or more than one new substance—is formed. The change is not reversible. For example, if you burn a piece of wood, two new substances are formed: smoke and ash. The smoke and ash cannot be turned back into wood. If you cook an egg, you cannot change the cooked egg back into a raw egg.

Signs of a Chemical Change

The following are signs that a chemical change is happening:

- **Change in color:** When leaves change color in autumn, they are going through a chemical change.
- **Change in odor:** You can tell that an egg is rotten because of the awful odor. A rotting egg is undergoing a chemical change.
- **A precipitate forms:** A precipitate is a solid that forms when certain liquids are mixed together. If you see a precipitate form, you know that a chemical change has happened.
- **A gas is produced:** When you mix certain substances together, the mixture will begin to bubble. The bubbles are made of a gas that is produced through a chemical change.

Identifying Physical and Chemical Changes

1. Cut out the cards below and arrange them in two columns—one for physical changes and one for chemical changes. Be prepared to explain your thinking.

PHYSICAL CHANGES	CHEMICAL CHANGES
Baking cookie dough	Molten lava hardening into rock
Bread becoming moldy	Cooking rice
Lighting a match	Cracking open an egg
Crumpling tin foil	Digesting food
Breaking a glass	Toasting bread

Experiment: Observing a Chemical Change

Mixing substances together sometimes causes a chemical change to take place. This type of chemical change is called a chemical reaction. In this experiment, you can observe a chemical reaction.

What You Need

- Partner to work with
- Clean plastic water bottle (single-serving size)
- Water
- Effervescent antacid tablet
- Paper towel
- Latex balloon about 10 in (30 cm) diameter when inflated
- Clock or timer

SAFETY ALERT

Do **not** eat any of the antacid tablet or drink the liquid in this experiment.

Getting Ready

1. Blow up the balloon and let the air out. (Make sure the balloon does not get so big that it breaks.) Repeat two or three times.
2. Practice putting the opening of the balloon over the mouth of the water bottle. (You and your partner will need to do this fairly quickly during the experiment. Decide now who will hold the bottle steady and who will put the balloon over the mouth of the bottle.)

What You Do

3. Pour water into the bottle until it is half full.
4. Over a paper towel, break the antacid tablet into several pieces. Drop the pieces into the bottle. (Be ready for the next step!)
5. Put the balloon over the mouth of the bottle. Notice how the balloon looks.
6. Wait for one minute and watch what happens. (If the balloon gets big enough to break, do the next step right away.)
7. Pinch the neck of the balloon and carefully pull it off the bottle. Slowly let the air out of the balloon.
8. Pour the liquid down the drain and throw out the balloon.

"Experiment: Observing a Chemical Change"—Think About It!

1. Draw a picture that shows how the balloon looked when you first put it over the mouth of the bottle. Then draw what the balloon looked like after one minute.

2. Most gases are invisible. In this experiment, what are two signs that a gas is produced from a chemical change?

____

____

____

____

3. When the balloon expands, is it going through a chemical change or a physical change? Why do you think so?

____

____

____

____

What is happening in this experiment?

The antacid tablet contains chemicals that react with each other, causing a chemical change. These chemicals do not react with each other when they are dry (as in the tablet), but they do react with each other when they are dissolved in water. A new substance—carbon dioxide gas—forms from the chemical change that takes place.

Breakfast Science

Write a menu for the ultimate breakfast. Beside each menu item, indicate whether preparing the food involves a physical change (P), or a chemical change (C). Explain your thinking. Create a draft using the planner below. Create a good copy of your breakfast menu on a separate piece of paper.

________________________________'s Ultimate Breakfast Menu

Food item: ____________________	**Type of Change: Circle P or C**
Describe the change	

Food item: ____________________	**Type of Change: Circle P or C**
Describe the change	

Food item: ____________________	**Type of Change: Circle P or C**
Describe the change	

Food item: ____________________	**Type of Change: Circle P or C**
Describe the change	

What Is So Great About Gases?

Lots of inventions that people use every day rely on gases.

Air Bags in Cars

Air bags save lives and prevent injuries. An air bag inflates when it is filled with nitrogen gas. How does an air bag work? A car contains a crash sensor that can detect when a crash has taken place. The crash sensor sends a signal to the air bag's inflator. In the inflator, two chemicals react with each other in a chemical change that produces nitrogen gas. As the nitrogen gas starts to fill the air bag, the bag pops out and fully inflates. Tiny holes in the air bag allow the gas to escape so the passenger is not trapped behind the air bag.

An air bag has to inflate at lightning speed if it is going to prevent injury. Air bags burst out of their storage site at a speed of over 186 mph (300 km/h). From the time a crash sensor detects a crash to when the air bag is fully inflated is only 1/25 of a second!

Aerosol Cans

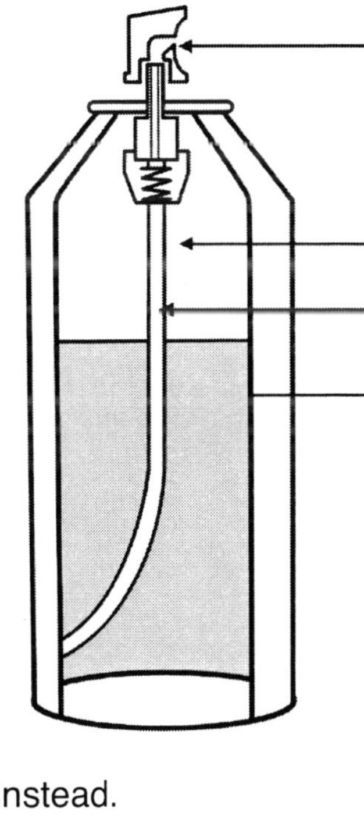

Room fresheners and hairspray are available in aerosol cans, sometimes called spray cans. Gas is what makes aerosol cans work.

An aerosol can has gas at the top and the product (such as hairspray) at the bottom. The gas pushes down on the product. Since the product has nowhere to go, nothing happens. When you press the nozzle, you create an opening so the product has somewhere to go. The pushing force of the gas makes the product rush up a plastic tube. The product comes out of the nozzle in a spray.

The gas used in some aerosol cans is harmful to the environment. Many people choose products in a pump container instead.

Fire Extinguishers

Most fire extinguishers use a chemical foam or powder to put out fires. One type of extinguisher uses a gas to put out fires. The tank of this extinguisher is filled with liquid carbon dioxide. When the extinguisher is activated, the liquid carbon dioxide changes to a gas as it sprays out.

Fire needs oxygen. A fire will go out if not enough oxygen is available. Carbon dioxide gas pushes the oxygen away. The fire goes out because there is not enough oxygen around it to keep it burning.

"What Is So Great About Gases?"—Think About It!

1. An air bag needs to fill evenly with gas so that all parts of the air bag can protect passengers from injury. (If any part did not inflate as much, it would offer less protection from injury.) Explain why airbags always fill evenly.

2. Since aerosol room fresheners can harm the environment, some people use air fresheners that are solids. Explain how solid air fresheners work. (**Hint:** Solid air fresheners work without melting.)

Brain Stretch

Balloons filled with helium gas float because helium is lighter than air. Over time, a helium balloon will slowly deflate, even if the opening at the end of the balloon is tightly tied. Come up with a theory to explain why helium balloons deflate. Then do some research to find out whether your theory is correct. (**Hint:** The helium gas in the balloon does not change to another state inside the balloon.)

Changes of State Review

Under the diagram, write the name of the process indicated by each numbered arrow. Tell whether heat is absorbed or released in each process.

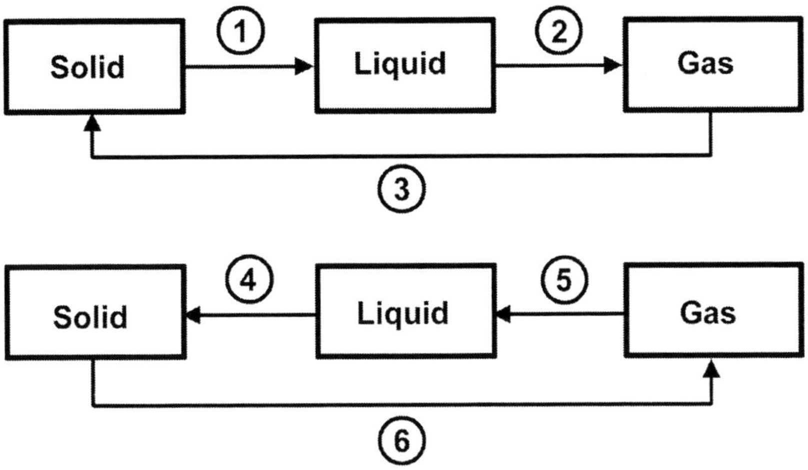

1. Process: ______________________

   Heat is ______________________ .

2. Process: ______________________

   Heat is ______________________ .

3. Process: ______________________

   Heat is ______________________ .

4. Process: ______________________

   Heat is ______________________ .

5. Process: ______________________

   Heat is ______________________ .

6. Process: ______________________

   Heat is ______________________ .

Matter Word Search

Solve each clue with one word. Then find the word in the word search puzzle.

1. Sublimation changes matter in this state into a gas. ______________________

2. The amount of space an object takes up. ______________________

3. When matter changes state, it is going through this type of change. ______________________

4. The term related to how easily a substance dissolves in liquid. ______________________

5. Matter in this state does not have a definite volume. ______________________

6. The amount of matter in an object. ______________________

7. The term related to how much a substance resists flowing. ______________________

8. This type of change in matter is not reversible. ______________________

Look also for these words related to the topic of matter:

liquid	**particles**	**property**	
dissolve	**state**	**freeze**	**deposition**

F	R	E	E	Z	E	V	Y	L	V	A	T	E
I	D	E	P	O	S	I	T	I	O	N	Y	U
Q	U	D	Y	G	O	S	I	P	L	D	C	L
P	T	I	W	O	Y	C	L	A	U	I	N	A
A	R	L	E	T	J	O	I	R	M	S	E	C
L	Y	O	M	A	S	S	B	T	E	S	B	I
G	A	S	P	A	T	I	U	I	D	O	R	M
S	T	A	T	E	O	T	L	C	X	L	O	E
E	O	U	K	M	R	Y	O	L	U	V	S	H
L	I	Q	U	I	D	T	S	E	R	E	B	C
E	C	A	F	D	P	H	Y	S	I	C	A	L

Natural Resources

Where did the paper this is printed on come from? What about the food you ate for breakfast, or the clothes you are wearing? Where does the electricity for the lights in your classroom come from? Everything that people use in their daily lives comes from Earth. We call these things natural resources because they come from nature. Some resources help us to stay alive. Others help us to live more enjoyable lives. Some are sources of energy.

Living and Non-living Resources

Natural resources can be living or non-living. Living things get energy from their environment to do things such as grow, move, and reproduce. A tree is a living thing. It uses water and sunlight to make energy so it can grow. A rock is a non-living thing. It does not use energy, and it does not grow or move on its own.

Fish are a very important living natural resource. Fish are a source of food for people. Water is a very important non-living natural resource. We use water for drinking, cooking, and washing. We also use water to make electricity. We use the electricity for energy to make many things work, such as the lights in our homes and schools.

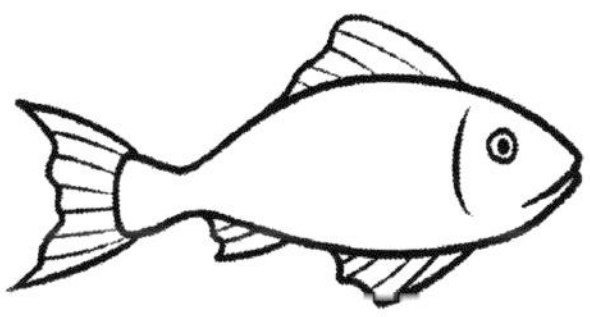

Renewable and Non-renewable Resources

Natural resources can also be renewable or non-renewable. Some renewable resources can be replaced or grown again. Trees are one example. Trees can reproduce themselves through seeds. Trees that are cut down can be replaced with seedlings. Seedlings are very young trees grown from seeds. Other renewable resources are always here for people to use. Wind is one example. Wind power is used to produce electricity.

Non-renewable resources cannot be replaced. They are non-renewable because they take a very long time to form. Fossil fuels and minerals are non-renewable resources. Oil is a fossil fuel. The oil we use today was formed millions of years ago. People use fossil fuels to produce energy. Oil can be made into gasoline to make cars and buses run.

"Natural Resources"—Think About It!

1. Complete the chart below with examples of living and non-living things. Try to list at least five for each category. Do not use examples from the text you have just read. Compare your chart with a classmate's. Do you agree with each other's examples?

Living Things	Non-living Things

2. Below is a list of natural resources. Beside each one, write whether it is renewable or non-renewable.

a) the Sun ____________________

b) coal ________________________

c) cotton plant _________________

d) copper _____________________

e) salmon ______________________

f) cow __________________________

g) gasoline ___________________________

h) ocean waves ___________________

3. Oil is used to make plastic bottles. Glass bottles are made from sand. Which of these could be called a renewable product? Why? Which is a non-renewable product? Why?

____

____

____

____

Using Resources

We use natural resources in many ways. We use some resources almost in their original form. We drink water and eat salmon. The water and the salmon are easy to identify. That is because they have not been changed into something else.

Products Made from Resources

Many resources are changed into products that we use. Sometimes it is easy to identify the resource that was used to make the product. Wood from trees is used to build houses and furniture. The wood in a bookcase looks like the wood in a tree. That is how we know it came from a tree. But wood can also be used to make paper, and paper does not look like wood.

Oil is a resource that is used in many different products. These include plastic containers, paint, soap, helmets, carpets, and tires. None of these look like the oil that comes from underground.

Different technologies are used to change resources into products. Before this can happen, the resources need to be harvested or extracted. Resources that are taken from Earth's surface are harvested. Resources that are taken from below Earth's surface are extracted. So trees are harvested, and oil is extracted.

From the Ground to Your Bathroom

Copper pipes are used for plumbing. You may have some copper pipes bringing water to the bathroom in your house. These are the steps for turning copper into copper pipes:

1. Ore containing copper is mined from below Earth's surface.
2. Ore is crushed, then ground into a powder.
3. The powder is concentrated so there is more copper in the mixture.
4. The copper mixture is smelted, or heated at high temperatures.
   This is done until it is 99 percent copper.
5. The copper is refined or made purer, then formed into big blocks.
6. Blocks are shipped to a manufacturer to make pipes.

That is one example of how we change a natural resource into a useful product.

"Using Resources"—Think About It!

1. Sometimes it is difficult to identify the resource a product was made from. Why?

2. a) Trees are harvested. Name two other resources that are harvested.

b) Oil and copper are extracted. Name two other resources that are extracted.

3. Copper ore and the copper used to make copper pipes are different. In what ways?

4. Below are the steps used to turn trees into the type of paper used in textbooks. Write the steps in the correct order in the flow chart.

- Bark is rubbed off the trees.
- Paper is coated to make finished paper.
- Logs are cut into chips.
- Paper is cut into sheets and packaged.
- Pulp is dried and pressed to make paper.
- Trees are cut down.
- Chips are cooked with chemicals to make pulp.
- Pulp is bleached to make it white.

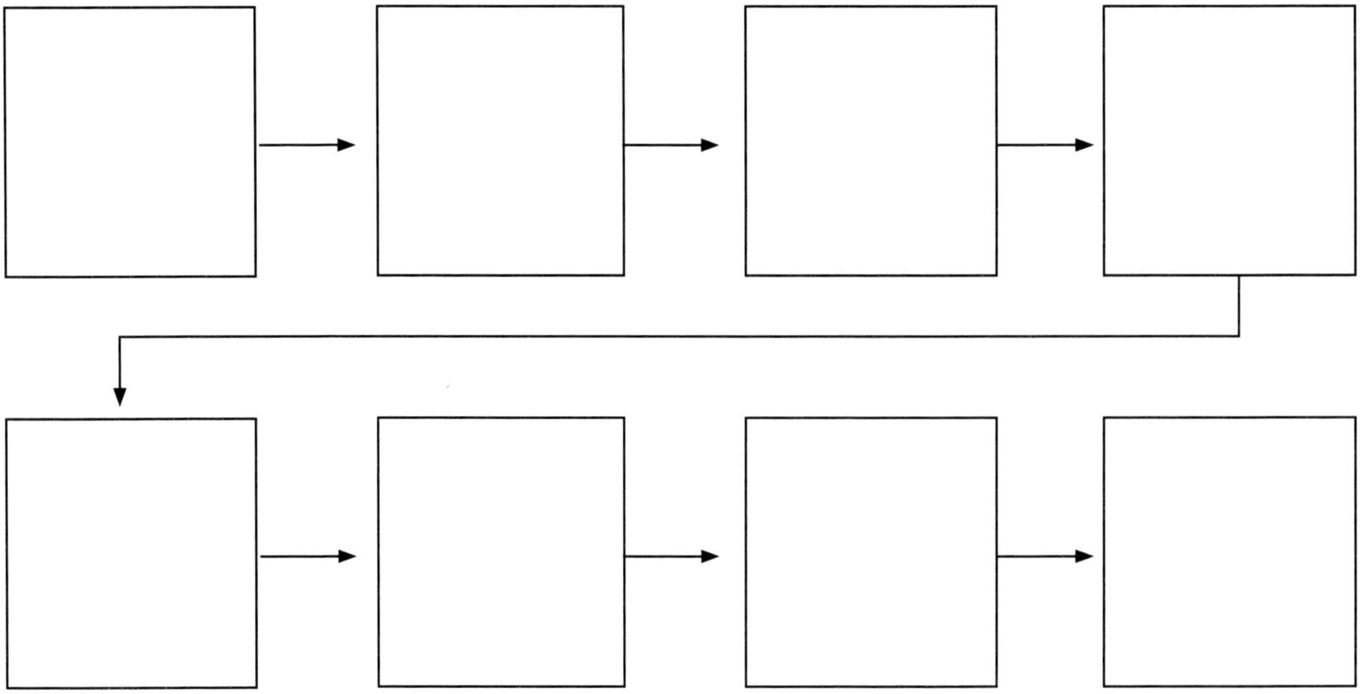

Conserving Resources

Conservation means using Earth's resources wisely and not wasting them. If people use resources too quickly, those resources might disappear. That means they will not be here for others to use in the future. Many governments, companies, and organizations now understand how important conservation is. So do people just like you. They try to do what they can to conserve resources. Write a persuasive paragraph to convince people about how important it is to conserve resources.

"Conserving Resources"—Think About It!

1. Three things that you can do to conserve resources are reduce, reuse, and recycle. By reducing, you use fewer resources and produce less garbage. When you reuse, you use the same product again or use it in a different way. Recycling is the third way to conserve. Many products can be recycled and made into new products. This includes things such as cans, paper, and glass.

   In the chart below, list what you could do to conserve resources. Try to list ten ideas for each column. Put a check mark beside the things that you already do.

I can reduce by...	I can reuse by...	I can recycle by...

Forms of Energy

Energy is the ability to do work. We use energy in everything we do. Our bodies use energy to grow. Cars use energy to move. Stoves use energy to cook food. Energy comes in many forms. Here are some examples:

- Chemical energy is energy that is stored in certain substances. Wood has chemical energy. When we burn wood, it releases its chemical energy.
- Motion energy or mechanical energy is motion that does work. Wind has motion energy. When wind moves, it can turn a windmill.
- Thermal energy is heat energy. We use heat energy to warm our homes.
- Electrical energy is movement, light, heat, or sound caused by electricity. Lightning is an example of electrical energy in nature. Electrical energy makes lightbulbs work.

Sources of Energy

We get energy from different sources. Some of these sources are renewable. Here are some examples of renewable energy sources:

- Biomass is energy from burning plants or garbage.
- Geothermal energy is heat energy from below Earth's surface.
- Hydropower is energy from moving water.
- Solar energy is energy from the Sun.
- Wind energy is energy from wind.

We use renewable energy sources mainly to make electricity.

Most of our sources of energy are non-renewable. These include oil, natural gas, and coal. We use these sources mainly to produce electricity, heat, and gasoline. Oil, coal, and natural gas are fossil fuels. This means they were formed millions of years ago.

"Forms of Energy"—Think About It!

1. Read the examples below. Beside each one, write the form of energy the example shows: chemical, motion, thermal, or electrical.

a) Throwing a bowling ball at the pins: ______________________

b) Water falling over a dam: ______________________

c) A battery in a flashlight: ______________________

d) Turning on a gas fireplace: ______________________

e) A computer plugged into a wall socket: ______________________

2. Why are the Sun, wind, and moving water considered to be renewable energy sources?

____

____

3. Why are fossil fuels non-renewable energy sources?

____

____

4. Do you think wind energy could be an important source of energy everywhere in the world? Why or why not?

____

____

5. Why do you think fossil fuels are our main sources of energy?

____

____

Word Stretch

The prefix "bio" in biomass means "life." The prefix "geo" in geothermal means "earth" or "ground." The prefix "hydro" in hydropower means "water." Find other words that start with each of these prefixes. What is the connection between each prefix and the meaning of each word?

Fossil Fuels

The three main fossil fuels are coal, oil, and natural gas. All of these were formed hundreds of millions of years ago, before the time of the dinosaurs.

When fossil fuels were formed, much of Earth was covered with swamps. The swamps were filled with trees, ferns, and other large leafy plants. The trees and plants died and sank to the bottom of the swamps. There they formed a spongy material called peat. Over many hundreds of years, sand, clay, and other minerals covered the peat. It slowly turned into rock. More and more rock was formed. The rock weighed down on the peat, squeezing all the water out of it. Over millions of years, the peat turned into coal, oil, and natural gas.

Oil also formed in the oceans. The ocean was full of tiny sea creatures called diatoms. When they died, they fell to the sea floor where they were slowly covered by rock. Over time, heat and pressure turned them into oil.

Where Are Fossil Fuels Found Today?

Several countries in the Middle East are among the world's largest oil producers. The United States, Canada, Russia, and China are also among the largest oil-producing countries. Oil is found on land, as well as in the oceans. There are a number of drilling platforms in the Gulf of Mexico. The largest reserves of coal are found in the United States, Russia, and China. Natural gas is usually found with oil or coal. There may also be many undiscovered fossil fuel reserves in the world.

How We Use Fossil Fuels

One of the main uses of fossil fuels is to make electricity. In the world, coal is the main fuel source for making electricity. Natural gas and oil are also used. Fossil fuels are also used to make fuels for vehicles. These fuels are mainly made from oil. The third main use for fossil fuels is for heating and cooling. Oil and natural gas are the main fuels used for this purpose.

"Fossil Fuels"—Think About It!

1. In the space below, make a flow chart to show how fossil fuels were formed.

2. Drills are used to get oil and natural gas from below Earth's surface. They make holes in the land or in the ocean floor. The oil or gas is then pumped out. Do you think it would be easier to drill on land or on the ocean floor? What are some problems that ocean drilling might present?

3. Natural gas has no odor. It is highly combustible, which means it burns easily. Before the gas is delivered for use, a chemical is added to give it an odor. Why do you think this is done?

How We Use Energy

The United States is a very developed country. We use a lot of energy in our homes, schools, businesses, and for transportation. The U.S. Energy Information Administration measures how much energy is used in four sectors:

Transportation Sector

This includes the vehicles that transport people or goods. Examples include vehicles such as cars, trucks, buses, trains, boats, aircraft, and subways.

Residential Sector

This includes all homes and apartments.

Commercial Sector

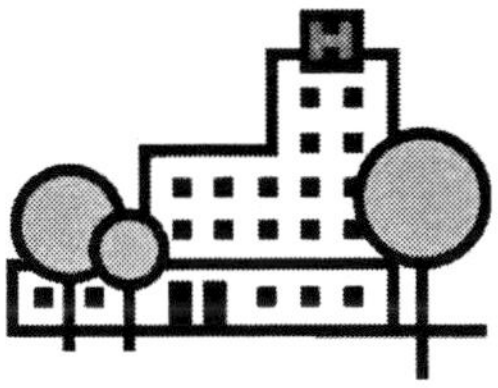

This includes buildings such as malls, stores, schools, office buildings, hospitals, restaurants, and warehouses.

Industrial Sector

This includes buildings and equipment used for manufacturing, agriculture, mining, forestry, and construction.

Did you know the industrial sector uses the most energy of all the sectors? It is responsible for about one-third of all energy consumed!

Energy Use in Our Homes

In the United States, natural gas and electricity are used to heat most homes, including apartment buildings. About 15 percent of all homes are heated through the use of other fuels such as oil, wood, wood pellets, or propane. We also use energy in our homes for other purposes, including

- lighting
- heating water
- appliances such as refrigerators and blenders
- electronic equipment such as televisions and computers

The amount of electricity used by appliances at home has doubled in the last 30 years!

"How We Use Energy"—Think About It!

1. Why do you think industry uses so much energy?

2. Some people use wood or propane to heat their homes. Where do you think these people might live? Why might they use these fuels instead of natural gas or electricity?

3. People use more energy in their homes today than they did 20 years ago. What might have caused this increase in energy use?

4. In which room of your home does your family use the most energy? Why?

How Does Energy Work?

You have learned that energy is the ability to do work. You have also learned that energy comes in many forms. Each form of energy is either kinetic or potential. Kinetic energy is the energy of something moving, such as waves, rays, objects, electrons, atoms, molecules, and substances. So blowing wind is kinetic energy. It is also motion or mechanical energy. Potential energy is stored energy. So a battery has potential energy as well as chemical energy.

One very important thing about energy is that it cannot be created or destroyed. So when we use energy, it does not disappear. It just changes from one form of energy to another. An example is when a car engine burns gasoline. The engine changes the chemical energy of the gasoline into motion energy. The motion energy makes the car run. Some of the chemical energy is also changed into thermal energy. That is why a car engine heats up. The chemical energy from the gasoline has been changed to motion energy and thermal energy.

Energy Transformations

When energy changes from one form to another, we call it energy transformation. Here are some examples of energy transformations and their uses:

- A television changes electrical energy into sound and light energy. As a result, you can see and hear the television shows.
- A flashlight battery changes chemical energy into light energy. As a result, you can use the flashlight to see in the dark.
- A phone changes sound energy from your voice into electrical energy. This electrical energy is then changed back into sound energy. As a result, the person on the other end of the phone can hear what you said.
- Solar panels change sunlight into electric energy.

Energy transformations produce useful energy (energy that does work). They also produce wasted energy (usually as heat or sound). Most energy transformations are not very efficient. This means they produce a lot of wasted energy. For example, your body changes the chemical energy in food to motion energy. This gives you the energy to move, breathe, and think. But your body is not very efficient at converting food into useful energy. Your body is less than 5 percent efficient most of the time. The rest of the energy is lost as heat.

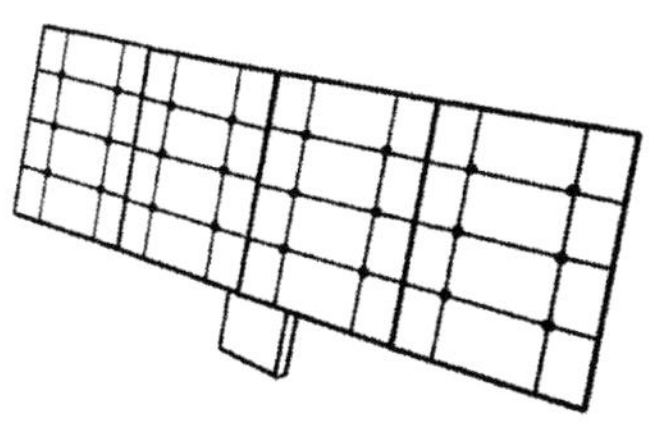

solar panel

"How Does Energy Work?"—Think About It!

1. Energy transformations make devices work so they can do things that help us. The alarm clock that wakes you up in the morning uses energy transformation. So does the bicycle you ride to school. Now it is your turn to design a device that will do a specific task. Your device can be something real, such as a child's toy. Or it can be something imaginary, such as a device that turns the pages of a book.

Here are some guidelines:

- You will not have to build the device, only design and sketch it.
- Your device must have at least one energy transformation.
- Your device must use materials that are readily available.

On another sheet of paper, draw your design. Then answer the following questions:

a) What is your device designed to do? ______________________________

____

b) Write a list of steps, in order, that explain how your device works. ______________________________

____

____

____

____

c) What energy transformation (or transformations) that will happen? When will it happen?

____

____

d) Was any energy wasted in your device? What type of energy was wasted? Where was it lost?

____

____

____

Share your design with a classmate. Talk about any improvements you could make to the device to make it work better.

Sources of Energy Brochure

Create a brochure on sources of energy!

STEP 1: Plan Your Brochure

- ❑ Take a piece of paper and fold the paper the same way your brochure will be folded. Before writing the brochure, plan the layout in pencil. Sections of the brochure should include
  - Descriptions of two types of renewable energy
  - Descriptions of two types of non-renewable energy
  - Advantages and disadvantages of each type of energy
  - How people use each type of energy
  - Interesting facts
- ❑ Write the heading for each section where you would like it to be in the brochure.
- ❑ Plan where graphics or pictures will be placed in the brochure.

STEP 2: Complete a Draft

- ❑ Research information for each section of your brochure. Check your facts.
- ❑ Read your draft for meaning, then add, delete, or change words to make your writing better.
- ❑ Plan what illustrations or graphics you will put into your brochure.

STEP 3: Checklist

- ❑ My brochure is neat and well organized.
- ❑ My brochure has accurate information.
- ❑ My brochure has pictures or graphics that go well with the information.
- ❑ I checked the spelling.
- ❑ I checked the punctuation.
- ❑ My brochure is attractive.

Energy Vocabulary

1. In each group of words below, circle the one that does not belong. On the line below the group of words, explain why the word does not belong.

a) reduce dump reuse recycle

____

b) coal natural gas biomass oil

____

c) kinetic chemical harvested gravitational

____

d) geothermal hydropower solar fossil fuels

____

2. Unscramble the letters to make "energy" words.

a) n b w e e l r e a ______________________

b) r c t x a e e d t ______________________

c) s r v c o i o n n e a t ______________________

d) t o e m p e u l r ______________________

e) f n a o r r t o n t s m i a ______________________

3. Write a definition for each of the unscrambled words from question 2.

a) ______________________________

____

b) ______________________________

____

c) ______________________________

____

d) ______________________________

____

e) ______________________________

____

Conserving Energy

We use energy every day. We use it to make our lives comfortable and enjoyable. But we must remember that the supply of energy is not limitless. To keep our way of life, we need to use our energy resources wisely. By saving energy ourselves, we can also help others in the world have a good life. Conserving will also make sure people in the future have energy for their needs.

New Technologies

Many new technologies have been developed that can help us save energy. Here are some examples:

- Electric and hybrid cars: These cars use less gasoline. They help reduce the amount of oil used.
- Plants as plastic: Plastic products can be made from plant materials. This will conserve oil, since most plastic is made from oil.
- Solar power plants to generate electricity: Solar energy will always be available. It is Earth's most available energy source. Using solar energy will conserve other energy sources.
- Compact fluorescent lightbulbs: These bulbs produce the same amount of light as incandescent bulbs. But they use less energy than incandescent bulbs. So compact fluorescent bulbs save electricity.

In the Home

Appliances such as stoves are the main source of energy use in homes. Other examples are washers, furnaces, and water heaters. Energy Star® is an American program that helps people buy appliances and equipment that use less electricity. This label is put on appliances and equipment that are the most energy efficient.

You Are Important

You can do many things to conserve energy. Think about all the things you do at home, at school, and everywhere else. How do you use energy? How could you reduce the energy you use? What help do you need from others to reduce energy use?

"Conserving Energy"—Think About It!

1. Write a persuasive paragraph on why it is important to save energy. Use information from the reading and your own ideas.

"Conserving Energy"—Think About It! (continued)

2. Which type of energy do you think it is more important to save: energy that comes from natural gas, or from hydropower? Why?

____

____

____

3. Solar energy technology is very expensive to build. This is one reason why it is not widely used yet. What might be another reason why it is not widely used?

____

____

____

4. You can help conserve energy. Below are some objects you might use or activities you might do. For each one, tell how you could use the object or do the activity to save energy. The first one is done for you.

a) Refrigerator: Do not stand with the door open while thinking about what you want to eat.

b) Lights in your bedroom: ______________________________

c) Hair dryer: ______________________________

d) Brushing your teeth: ______________________________

e) Washing clothes: ______________________________

f) Taking a bath: ______________________________

g) Television: ______________________________

h) Computer: ______________________________

i) Dishwasher: ______________________________

j) Going to school: ______________________________

Share your ideas with a classmate.

The Impact of Resource and Energy Use

It is important to conserve natural resources so they will available for future use. But there are other things to think about when it comes to resource and energy use. Resource and energy use can have an impact on people and the environment in many ways.

The harvesting or extracting of natural resources can have an impact. For example, open-pit mines are used to mine many types of minerals. This means that huge holes are dug in the land to find the minerals. These mines can pollute rivers and streams. They can also add to air pollution. Logging forests (cutting down the trees) can also have impacts. Habitats for plants and animals can be destroyed. When trees are cut, soil can be washed away by heavy rain. Resources are turned into useful items in processing plants. These plants can also add to air and water pollution. They also use very large amounts of energy.

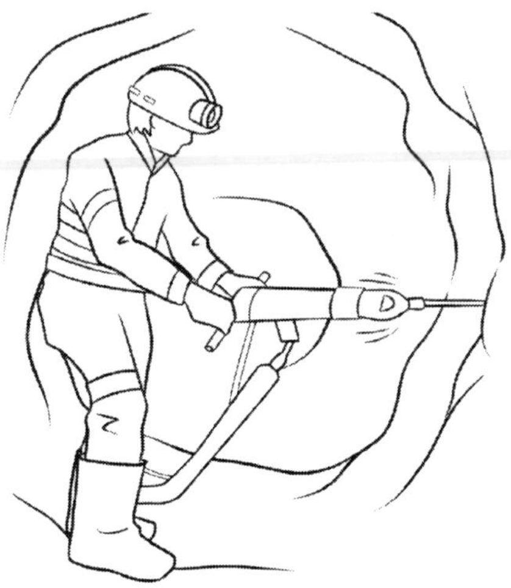

mining

In the United States, people are very concerned about damaging the environment. All levels of government have laws to protect the environment. These laws make sure companies lessen their impact on the environment. Companies often develop new procedures to help in this effort.

Consultation

How are decisions made about resource production? For example, what happens when a company wants to open a mine? One of the most important things that happens is consultation. This means that people get together to give their opinions and ideas. These people may include scientists, environmentalists, politicians, people from the company, and people from the community. Sometimes these consultations can go on for years before a decision is made.

The final decision is made by either the state or federal government, or both. To make the decision, the government considers the benefits of the project, as well as the concerns. The resource produced by a mine might be in great demand. If the resource is in demand, the economy of the community will improve. This could mean more jobs for people in the community. It could also mean more money for things such as schools and hospitals.

"The Impact of Resource and Energy Use"—Think About It!

Everyone Has an Opinion

A large electric company wants to build a dam and power plant to generate electricity. On the negative side, building the dam and plant will change the environment. They will have to move lots of earth and build roads. A huge amount of land behind the dam will be flooded to create a reservoir. The normal flow of the river will be stopped. This would affect the plants and fish in the river. Tourists visit the area because it has beautiful scenery. They also like to fish in the river. If the dam is built, tourism will probably be affected.

On the positive side, the power plant will produce clean and inexpensive power. This power can be sold to bring money into the community. Right now, there are only a few tourism jobs for people in the town near the river. Many people have moved away. Building the dam will mean lots of jobs.

1. Think about the following people and the opinions they might have. Decide whether each one would support or oppose the dam. Give reasons for your ideas.

a) People from the town who need jobs: ______________________________

____

____

b) Scientists who are concerned about the impact on the environment: ______________

____

____

c) The local town government: ______________________________

____

____

d) People from nearby communities who want cheaper electricity: ______________

____

____

e) People who fish in the river: ______________________________

____

____

Take One Point of View

Read the statement. It is important for government to consult many different people on projects such as building a dam and power plant to generate electricity.

1. Do you agree or disagree with this statement? Use the outline below to plan your writing.

A Statement of Your Point of View	
Main Idea	**Supporting Evidence**
Main Idea	**Supporting Evidence**
Main Idea	**Supporting Evidence**

STEM-Related Occupations

To learn more about some of these occupations visit the following websites:

http://www.sciencebuddies.org/science-fair-projects/science_careers.shtml

http://kids.usa.gov/watch-videos/jobs/index.shtml

Accountant
Aerospace Engineer
Agricultural Engineer
Agricultural Technician
Aircraft Mechanic and Service Technician
Animal Breeder
Animal Trainer
Animator
Anthropologist
Architect
Astronaut
Astronomer
Athletic Trainer
Audio Engineer
Audiologist
Automotive Mechanic
Biochemical Engineer
Biochemist/Biophysicist
Biologist
Biology Teacher
Biomedical Engineer
Business Owner
Cardiovascular Technician
Carpenter
Chef
Chemical Engineer
Chemical Technician
Chemistry Teacher
Chiropractor
Civil Engineer
Civil Engineering Technician
Climate Change Analyst
Clinical Psychologist
Computer Engineer
Computer Programmer
Computer Systems Analyst
Construction Manager
Counseling Psychologist
Dietetic Technician
Dietitian and Nutritionist
Doctor
Electrical Engineering Technician
Electrician
Electronics Engineer
Emergency Medical Technician
Environmental Engineer
Environmental Engineering Technician
Environmental Restoration Planner
Environmental Scientist
Epidemiologist
Fire-Prevention Engineer
Fish and Game Worker
Food Science Technician
Food Scientist and Technologist
Forest and Conservation Technician
Forest and Conservation Worker
Geoscientist
Graphic Designer
Hydrologist
Industrial Engineer
Interior Designer
Landscape Architect
Manufacturing Engineer
Marine Architect
Marine Biologist
Math Teacher
Mechanical Engineer
Mechanical Engineering Technician
Medical Lab Technician
Medical Scientist
Meteorologist
Microbiologist
Microsystems Engineer
Mining and Geological Engineer
Molecular and Cellular Biologist
Neurologist
Nuclear Engineer
Nursery and Greenhouse Manager
Nutritionist
Occupational Health and Safety Specialist
Optical Engineer
Optometrist
Paleontologist
Patent Lawyer
Pathologist
Park Ranger
Petroleum Engineer
Pharmacist
Physical Therapist
Physician
Physician Assistant
Physicist
Pilot
Psychologist
Registered Nurse
Respiratory Therapist
Robotics Engineer or Technician
School Psychologist
Seismologist
Software Developer (Applications)
Software Developer (Systems Software)
Soil and Plant Scientist
Soil and Water Conservationist
Space Scientist
Speech-Language Pathologist
Statistician
Transportation Engineer
Transportation Planner
Urban Planner
Veterinarian
Video Game Designer
Volcanologist
Water/Wastewater Engineer
Wind Energy Engineer
X-Ray Technician
Zoo Keeper
Zoologist and Wildlife Biologist

Science, Technology, Engineering, and Mathematics (STEM) Occupation Brochure

Create a brochure about a STEM-related occupation.

STEP 1: Plan Your Brochure

- [ ] Take a piece of paper and fold the paper the same way your brochure will be folded. Before writing the brochure, plan the layout in pencil. Sections of the brochure should include
  - Job description
  - Training or degree needed
  - Work environment
  - How the occupation relates to STEM
  - Interesting facts
- [ ] Write the heading for each section where you would like it to be in the brochure.
- [ ] Plan where graphics or pictures will be placed in the brochure.

STEP 2: Complete a Draft

- [ ] Research information for each section of your brochure. Check your facts.
- [ ] Read your draft for meaning, then add, delete, or change words to make your writing better.
- [ ] Plan what illustrations or graphics you will put into your brochure.

STEP 3: Checklist

- [ ] My brochure is neat and well organized.
- [ ] My brochure has accurate information.
- [ ] My brochure has pictures or graphics that go well with the information.
- [ ] I checked the spelling.
- [ ] I checked the punctuation.
- [ ] My brochure is attractive.

What Does a Marine Biologist Do?

Marine Biologists

Biologists study living things, including plants and animals. A marine biologist is someone who studies plants and animals that live in the ocean. Thousands of different plants and animals live in the ocean, so many marine biologists choose to study just one thing. For example, a marine biologist might decide to study dolphins, sharks, or seaweed.

Where Marine Biologists Do Their Work

Some marine biologists work on a boat. They might watch whales that come to the ocean's surface and observe how they behave and where they travel. Marine biologists might also use underwater cameras to watch animals that do not come to the surface.

Other marine biologists go down into the ocean. Some are scuba divers who collect underwater plants so they can learn more about them. The scuba divers might also collect marine animals. They study the animals to learn about how their bodies work and whether they have any diseases.

Sometimes marine biologists use a small type of submarine to go into the ocean. The submarine has bright lights and lots of clear plastic so people can see what is happening under the ocean's surface.

Some marine biologists work in laboratories, observing fish in large water tanks, or looking at tiny sea creatures under a microscope.

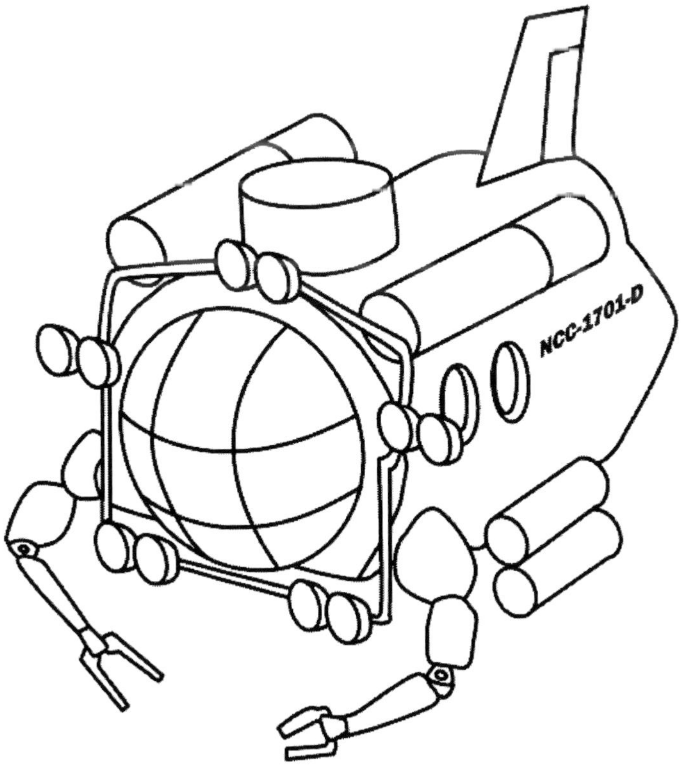

This small submarine has lots of lights for seeing things in deep water, and claws for picking things up off the ocean floor.

Becoming a Marine Biologist

If you are interested in becoming a marine biologist, learn to read and write well. Marine biologists read and write many scientific reports. You should also work hard at science. People take lots of science courses at university to become marine biologists.

"What Does a Marine Biologist Do?" — Think About It

1. Write a definition for marine animals.

2. Different types of scientists often become experts in one particular topic. Is this true of marine biologists? Give evidence from the article to support your answer.

3. Some marine biologists do not go down into the ocean. What are three examples of ways these marine biologists study animals?

4. Scuba divers and small submarines cannot stay underwater for very long periods of time. Why?

5. The illustration shows a small submarine that marine biologists might use. Write two things you learned about this submarine from the illustration.

6. What is one way that marine biologists share the information they learn?

What Does a Carpenter Do?

A carpenter uses tools to join together pieces of wood to build structures.

Getting Started

Before carpenters can start building, they need to have a plan to follow. The plan is a diagram of the structure they are going to build. The diagram gives all the measurements of the structure. Carpenters use the plan to figure out how much wood they will need, what size and shape each piece of wood needs to be, and what tools will be needed.

Battery powered drill

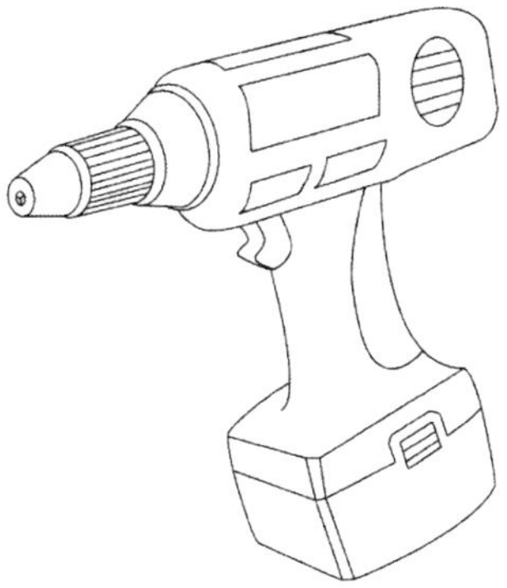

Building with Tools

Carpenters use power tools and hand tools. Power tools get their power from electricity. Examples of power tools are electric saws, drills, and sanders. Hand tools do not use electricity. Carpenters use their muscles for power when they use hand tools such as hammers and hand saws.

Handsaw

Types of Carpenters

Carpenters are divided into different categories, depending on the type of work they do. Construction carpenters work on building large structures, such as new homes, office buildings, and stores. Residential carpenters work on homes that have already been built. They might put new wood floors in a house, repair the roof, or add a deck to the back of the house. Furniture makers build different types of wooden furniture. For example, if you want new kitchen cupboards, a bookshelf, or a table, a furniture maker can make what you need in the exact size and shape that you want.

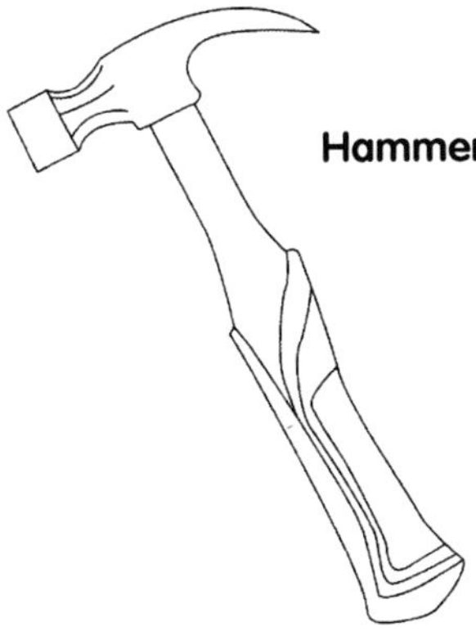

Hammer

Skills

Here are some examples of skills that carpenters need:

- Math skills: Carpenters use math skills when they add, subtract, multiply, or divide different measurements.
- Safety skills: Carpenters need to know how to use tools safely.
- Drawing skills: When furniture makers design a new piece of furniture, they make a drawing to show the customer what it will look like.

"What Does a Carpenter Do?" — Think About It

1. All carpenters use nails, screws, and glue. Why are these materials important in any carpenter's job?

____

____

2. The article mentions electric saws, drills, and sanders. Why did the author provide these examples of tools?

____

____

3. Power tools need electricity to work. Hand tools also need a source of energy to do work. Where does this energy come from?

____

____

4. Which kind of carpenter would you need for each of the projects below?

Building a bridge: ______________________________

Replacing a home's old staircase: __________________________

5. The word *residential* comes from the word *residence.* Use information from the article to help you write a definition of residence.

____

____

6. How is putting together a wooden bookshelf from a store similar to and different from a furniture maker's job?

Similar: ____________________________________

____

Different: ___________________________________

____

The Computer Revolution

Today, everyone knows computers are machines and we depend on them in countless ways every day. But did you know that back in the early 1600s people were already using the word "computer"? Back in those days, it meant someone who did calculations, or computations. Computers have changed a lot since then.

The First Computer

Computers are machines that can be programmed to carry out sequences of logical or mathematical operations. Computer-like machines were first designed as long ago as the early 1800s, but none of them were ever built then.

Most experts agree that the first computer was not actually built until 1939. It was called the Atanasoff-Berry Computer, or ABC, after its American inventors, John Vincent Atanasoff and Clifford Berry. This computer couldn't be programmed, as computers today can be, but it was a start.

Scientists worked to make the computer programmable—this was the computer's software. But they also experimented to improve the actual machine, which was the computer's hardware. By 1946, they had created ENIAC, the first programmable computer. It could spit out results 1,000 times faster than other machines of the time!

Scientists in England were working on improving computer software. In 1948, they created a computer they called "Baby." It was the first computer that could store program instructions in its memory.

From Big to Little

One of the main ways that early computers differ from the ones you use today is that the old machines were huge. Computers such as ENIAC were more than twice as big as a classroom.

Computers had to be so big because they were powered by large glass tubes called vacuum tubes. Not only did these tubes become very hot when they were working, but they also did not work very well. Although there might be thousands of vacuum tubes in a single computer, if one burned out, the entire computer would stop working.

That all changed in the late 1950s when transistors began replacing the vacuum tubes. Transistors are tiny devices that are used to increase and change electronic signals and electrical power. They are much smaller and lighter than vacuum tubes. Transistors are also cheaper to make, more durable, and much more reliable.

Your Life with Computers

Thanks to transistors, computers became much smaller, more reliable, and more powerful. But scientists kept working to improve computers. They figured out how to put hundreds of transistors on an even smaller microchip. Suddenly computers became much smaller and much more powerful.

Without the computer, there would be no Internet, personal computers, World Wide Web, or many other technologies. In fact, most machines you use today are powered by computers.

"The Computer Revolution"—Think About It

1. Do you like playing computer games? Why or why not?

____

____

____

2. List all the ways that you have used computers today.

____

____

____

3. Inventor Thomas Edison once said, "Genius is 1% inspiration and 99% perspiration." What do you think this means?

____

____

____

4. What are some advantages of having smaller computers?

____

____

____

STEM Expert!

You are incredible!

Great Work!

Keep up the effort!

STEM Rubric

	Level 1 Below Expectations	Level 2 Approaches Expectations	Level 3 Meets Expectations	Level 4 Exceeds Expectations
Knowledge of STEM Concepts	• Displays little understanding of concepts. • Rarely gives complete explanations. • Intensive teacher support is needed.	• Displays a satisfactory understanding of most concepts. • Sometimes gives appropriate, but incomplete explanations. • Teacher support is sometimes needed.	• Displays a considerable understanding of most concepts. • Usually gives complete or nearly complete explanations. • Infrequent teacher support is needed.	• Displays a thorough understanding of all or almost all concepts. • Consistently gives appropriate and complete explanations independently. • No teacher support is needed.
Application of STEM Concepts	• Relates science concepts to outside world with extensive teacher prompts. • Application of concepts rarely appropriate and accurate.	• Relates science concepts to outside world with some teacher prompts. • Application of concepts sometimes appropriate and accurate.	• Relates science concepts to outside world with few teacher prompts. • Application of concepts usually appropriate and accurate.	• Relates science concepts to outside world independently. • Application of concepts almost always appropriate and accurate.
Written Communication of Ideas	• Expresses ideas with limited critical thinking skills. • Few ideas are well organized and effective.	• Expresses ideas with some critical thinking skills. • Some ideas are well organized and effective.	• Expresses ideas with considerable critical thinking skills. • Most ideas are well organized and effective.	• Expresses ideas with in-depth critical thinking skills. • Ideas are well organized and effective.
Oral Communication of Ideas	• Rarely uses correct science terminology when discussing science concepts.	• Sometimes uses correct science terminology when discussing science concepts.	• Usually uses correct science terminology when discussing science concepts.	• Consistently uses correct science terminology when discussing science concepts.

Notes: ______________________________

____

____

STEM Focus ____________________

Student's Name	Knowledge of STEM Concepts	Application of STEM Concepts	Written Communication of Ideas	Oral Communication Skills	Overall Mark

Unit: Human Body Systems

Your Respiratory System, pages 2–4

1. a) nose and mouth
b) nasal cavity
c) pharynx
d) larynx
e) trachea
f) bronchioles
g) alveoli

2. When you have a cold, your nose and throat are more sensitive and congested. That makes you sneeze, cough, and develop a sore throat. Your nose tries to keep germs out of your throat. To do this, it makes more mucus than usual and that is why your nose runs.

Experiment: How Much Air? page 5

1. Answers will vary.

2. In step 3, the air breathed into the bottle pushes water out of the bottle. The volume of the air that went into the bottle is equal to the volume of water pushed out. It also takes the same volume of water to refill the bottle.

Your Circulatory System, pages 6–7

1. a) Answers will vary.
b) Answers will vary.
c) The active pulse should be a higher number.

2. a) The neck pulse is stronger than the wrist pulse.
b) Students should feel the neck pulse first.
c) The artery in your neck is larger than the one in your wrist. This is one reason the pulse is stronger. Also, your neck is closer to your heart than your wrist is. That makes the pulse in your neck stronger. That also means you feel it slightly sooner than you feel it in your wrist. The blood gets to your neck faster than it gets to your wrist.

Your Digestive System, pages 8–9

1. a) mouth
b) esophagus
c) stomach
d) small intestine
e) large intestine
f) rectum

2. esophagus, small intestine, large intestine, and rectum

3. Sample answers: teeth—candy corn; esophagus—toilet paper tube; stomach—baggie; small intestine—ramen noodles; large intestine—hose; liver, pancreas, and gall bladder—modeling clay or rubber foam

4. a) The front teeth because they are sharpest.
b) The side and back teeth because they are flat and can grind food between them.

Your Bones and Skeleton, page 10

Sample answers:

1. a) elbow; b) hip; c) neck

2. The bones in my legs support my hips and upper body.

3. The skull protects the brain.

4. Bones support your body and joints help the parts bend.

The Muscles of Your Body, pages 11–12

1. a) Sample answers: athlete; boxer; construction worker; delivery person; dog walker; farmer; firefighter; lifeguard; soldier; personal trainer
b) Sample answers: sitting up straight; walking from place to place; reaching for objects; typing; moving a computer mouse

3. diaphragm

4. Muscle on front of arm (biceps).

5. Muscle on back of arm (triceps).

6. heart

Your Nervous System, pages 13–16

1. Descriptions should include the nerves reacting, observing, making motion, and maintaining the body (e.g., breathing and heart beating).

Experiment 1: Students should catch the ruler more quickly as they become more familiar with the experiment. In dim light, reflexes will likely be slower. Students cannot see the ruler as well in dim light.

Experiment 2: Results will vary.

Experiment 3: Crossing your fingers confuses your brain. Your brain does not usually receive these type of signals from your fingers. You make your brain think you must be feeling two separate things.

Sunlight and Vitamin D, pages 17–18

Sample answers:

1. wear sunscreen; cover your skin; limit time in sunlight; stay indoors during hottest time of day

2. exercise outside; meet with friends for an outdoor activity; read outside; help with outside chores; eat a meal outside; go for walks

3. Advantages—get vitamin D your body needs for strong bones and disease prevention; you are outside breathing fresh air; you are likely moving and getting exercise; sunshine makes most people feel happier
Disadvantages—sunburn damages your skin (may lead to cancer); overheating; dehydration

Healthy Eating: Journal Topics, page 19

Look for evidence that students are using the information they learned to make reasoned arguments.

Fitness and Health, pages 20–21

1. Sample answer: Eat nutritious food; drink a lot of water; exercise daily; get enough sleep; wear protective equipment; do not smoke; use sunscreen; get enough sunlight
2. Sample answer: more energy, healthier body, healthier heart, breathing easier, stronger muscles, fun

Create a Human Body Board Game, page 22

Answers will vary. Encourage students to test their board games with a partner to receive feedback.

Unit: Forces Acting on Structures and Mechanisms

Two Basic Forces: Pushing and Pulling, pages 23–24

1. a) You push the mouse from side to side to move the cursor back and forth. You push the mouse away from you to move the cursor up. You pull the mouse toward you to move the cursor down.
   b) You push and pull on the toothbrush to move it back and forth across your teeth. You push the brush against your teeth to apply light pressure.
   c) You push down on the pedals to move forward. To turn, you push the handlebars with one hand and pull with the other. To stop, you pull or squeeze the brake levers. To change gears, you push or pull the gear shifters.
2. Sample answer: In volleyball, you push the ball to serve. You also push the ball to send it back over the net during play. Gravity pulls the ball toward the ground.
3. Shape: The pushing force causes a change in the shape of the balloon by forcing it to become larger and more rounded.

Forces and Structures, pages 25–26

1. a) dead load; pipes do not move and never leave
   b) dead load; the elevator is permanently attached; the passengers are a live load
   c) live load; workers move and can leave
   d) live load; wind does not blow all the time
   e) dead load; balconies are permanently attached to the structure

Four Types of Internal Forces, pages 27–28

1. Compression; the weight of Ling's body pushes down on the mattress, squeezing it. The height of the mattress (when horizontal) becomes thinner.
2. a) Tension is acting on the strings. The tuning pegs pull on the strings. The strings stretch when Rick makes them tighter.
   b) Rick turns the tuning pegs. Torsion is acting on the pegs. Torsion is a twisting or turning force.
3. Bending acts on the wire. Maria and Marco must bend the wire to make it into a circular shape. Bending involves compression and tension.
4. Tension acts on the fishing line because it is being pulled from both ends. Mr. Green pulls on one end as he reels in the line. The fish pulls on the other end as it tries to swim away.

Experimenting with Materials and Forces, pages 29–30

Answers will vary as the rating scale is subjective. You might ask students to compare their results for different items or with a classmate.

Forces and Shapes, pages 31–32

1. compression
2. a) compression
   b) tension
3. a) The weight of the snow will push down on the roof, possibly causing it to bend or collapse.
   b) A triangular roof would be safer. The sloped sides of the roof make it easier for snow to slide off. (Gravity will pull it down to the ground.) Snow will not slide off a flat roof. The weight of snow might cause a flat roof to collapse.
   c) Rain will quickly run off the roof.
4. a) a dome and an arch
   b) Create buttresses of snow against the two sides of the arch.

Four Types of Bridges, pages 33–34

1. External, because they are temporary.
2. a) Compression acts on the blocks. The weight of the person on the bridge is transferred through the plank to the blocks. It pushes down on the blocks.
   b) Bending, or compression on the top of the plank and tension on the bottom.
   c) Internal, because it is part of the structure.
3. a) It tells you how much weight the bridge will have to support for each bus.
   b) It tells you the maximum weight the bridge may have to support.

Plastic Straw Bridge Challenge, page 35

Designs will vary. Look for evidence that students considered the strength of shapes and style of bridges.

Watch Out for Wind! pages 36–37

1. Sample answers: Most basements are built below the ground. So the force of the wind will not push on the basement walls. There is little danger that wind will cause basement walls to collapse.
2. The blanket helps protect you from flying glass and other debris.
3. The pointed rings of the nails will grab onto the surrounding wood. This helps to prevent the nail from being pulled out of the boards.
4. The rounded shape of a dome home allows wind to flow around and over it. So less force would push on a dome than would push on a house with straight walls.

Protect Yourself! pages 38–39

1. Goalies block shots with their legs. The thick pads protect the goalie's legs from the force of a fast-moving puck.
2. a) When you run, your feet hit the ground with greater force than when you walk. The impact or shock can cause injury. Cushioned soles help to absorb some of the impact.
   b) Compression is created when body weight pushes the shoe against the ground. The soles bend because the back of the shoe is lifted off the ground before the front. Soles that do not hold up under these forces will crack and break.
3. In a tight helmet, your head is already causing compression on the foam. The compressed foam then provides less protection to the wearer. Because of this, it cannot absorb as much compression from outside forces.
4. Gravity makes objects speed up as they approach Earth. So a skateboarder who is standing will hit the ground with a lot of force. But a skateboarder who is low to the ground will hit the ground with less force. This skateboarder will likely have less serious injuries than they would if they were standing.

Structures and the Environment, pages 40–41

1. Sample answers: damages the area that the materials are taken from; transporting and processing materials makes pollution, the construction process damages the area around them.
2. Sample answers: The ferry's engine will burn gasoline, which causes air pollution. Gasoline and oil from the ferry could leak into the river. This would affect plants and fish. The noise of the ferry's engine and propeller could affect fish and plant populations.
3. a) They would likely want a bridge because it could provide them with construction jobs.
   b) They would likely want the bridge because a ferry would disturb the fish and could damage the habitat.

Forces and Structures Quiz, page 42

1. speed, direction, shape
2. The pulling force of gravity makes the ball slow down as it travels upward. Eventually, the ball will change direction and gravity will pull it back to Earth. The ball will travel faster as it gets closer to Earth.
3. External forces come from things that are not part of the structure. Internal forces act within the structure.
4. a) torsion
   b) bending
   c) tension
   d) compression
5. Sample answer: triangle, dome
6. Answers will vary.

Unit: Properties of and Changes in Matter

What Is Matter? pages 43–44

1. All examples are made of matter.
2. a) B
   b) The two objects might not contain the same number of particles (or amount of matter).
3. a) a watermelon
   b) a quarter
4. a) volume
   b) greater (more) volume

Properties of Matter, pages 45–46

1. Sample answers: It is soft so it does not scratch skin or dishes; it can easily change shape to make drying a person or dish easier; and it does not dissolve in water.
2. a) a high viscosity
   b) Sample answer: red, sweet, cold, liquid
3. It allows you to see the food through the wrap.
4. a) The powder did not dissolve well and most of it settled to the bottom of the glass.
5. Sample answer: hard, writing height, brown, metal

Experiment: Do All Liquids Dissolve in Water? pages 47–48

1–6. Observations may vary. The alcohol and corn syrup should appear to dissolve. But the vegetable oil will not dissolve. It will float on top of the water.

7. No, not all liquids dissolve in water.

States of Matter, pages 49–50

1. Solid—a pencil, an elastic band
   Liquid—a drop of water, ink in a marker, flowing lava
   Gas—oxygen in the air, steam from hot soup
2. a) False
   b) False
   c) False
   d) The substance must be a gas because it does not have a definite volume. It can also expand to take up more space without changing state. Solids and liquids cannot do this.
3. a) a gas
   b) The gas has spread out to fill its container (the elevator). So the scent (which is a property of the gas) is the same strength throughout the elevator.

Experiment: What State Is It In? pages 51–52

Explanatory note: Shaving foam is made of liquid soap. It has many gas bubbles mixed into it. The gas adds stiffness to the liquid soap. It also helps the foam keep its shape. This is why it can support the penny. After being exposed to the air for two or three days, the gas escapes into the air and leaves behind solid soap. It also leaves tiny spaces where the gas bubbles were. Fresh shaving foam is a liquid combined with a gas. The shaving foam left in the open for two or three days is a solid.

Changes in States of Matter, pages 53–55

1. a) gas, liquid
   b) solid, melting
   c) gas
   d) deposition
   e) evaporation
   f) liquid, solid
   g) absorbed
   h) absorbed
   i) released
   j) released
   k) absorbed
   l) released
2. a) evaporation
   b) deposition
   c) freezing

Physical Changes and Chemical Changes, pages 56–57

1. Physical changes—Molten lava hardening into rock; Cracking open an egg; Crumpling tin foil; Breaking a glass.
   Chemical changes—Baking cookie dough; Bread becoming moldy; Cooking rice; Lighting a match; Digesting food; Toasting bread

Experiment: Observing a Chemical Change, pages 58–59

1. Pictures should show a flat balloon on the left and a very inflated balloon on the right.
2. Bubbles form in the liquid and the balloon inflates.
3. The balloon is going through a physical change because the change can be reversed—the balloon can be deflated.

Breakfast Science, page 60

Sample answer:
Orange Juice—melting and mixing (p)
Scrambled eggs—cracking and mixing (p), frying (c)
Toast—toasting (c), slicing (p)
Bacon—frying (c)
Pancakes—mixing (p), frying (c)
Oatmeal—heating in water (p)

What Is So Great About Gases? pages 61–62

1. A gas will spread out to fill its container (the air bag).
2. The solid air freshener changes state to become a gas. It gives off a scent and the scent spreads out to fill the room. This is because a gas spreads out to fill its container. The air freshener changes from a solid into a gas without first becoming a liquid (melting). So the air freshener goes through the process of sublimation.

Brain Stretch, page 62

The material the balloon is made from contains microscopic holes. The particles of helium gas escape through these holes over time. (Helium balloons are often made from a foil material. That is because foil contains fewer microscopic holes than latex does. A foil balloon will deflate more slowly than a latex balloon.)

Changes of State Review, page 63

1. melting, absorbed
2. evaporation, absorbed
3. deposition, released
4. freezing (or solidification), released
5. condensation, released
6. sublimation, absorbed

Matter Word Search, page 64

1. solid
2. volume
3. physical
4. solubility
5. gas
6. mass
7. viscosity
8. chemical

F	R	E	E	Z	E	V	Y	L	V	A	T	E
I	D	E	P	O	S	I	T	I	O	N	Y	U
Q	U	D	Y	G	O	S	I	P	L	D	C	L
P	T	I	W	O	Y	C	L	A	U	I	N	A
A	R	L	E	T	J	O	I	R	M	S	E	C
L	Y	O	M	A	S	S	B	T	E	S	B	I
G	A	S	P	A	T	I	U	I	D	O	R	M
S	T	A	T	E	O	T	L	C	X	L	O	E
E	O	U	K	M	R	Y	O	L	U	V	S	H
L	I	Q	U	I	D	T	S	E	R	E	B	C
E	C	A	F	D	P	H	Y	S	I	C	A	L

Unit: Conservation of Energy and Resources

Natural Resources, pages 65–66

1. Sample answer: Living Things—leaves, birds, frogs, snails, grass
   Non-living Things—soil, volcanoes, gold, aluminum, mountains
2. a) renewable
   b) non-renewable
   c) renewable
   d) non-renewable
   e) renewable
   f) renewable
   g) non-renewable
   h) renewable
3. Glass bottles are a renewable product. Sand is always being formed through the erosion of rock. So sand is a renewable resource. Plastic bottles are a non-renewable product. They are made from oil, which is a non-renewable resource.

Using Resources, pages 67–68

1. The products do not look like the resources they are made from.
2. Sample answers:
   a) Any fish or seafood, any plants, any animals
   b) Any minerals, coal, natural gas
3. Copper ore contains copper, but it also contains other things. Copper used to make pipes is pure copper.
4. Step should be in the following order:
   1)Trees are cut down.
   2) Bark is rubbed off the trees.
   3) Logs are cut into chips.
   4) Chips are cooked with chemicals to make pulp.
   5) Pulp is bleached to make it white.
   6) Pulp is dried and pressed to make paper.
   7) Paper is coated to make finished paper.
   8) Paper is cut into sheets and packaged.

Conserving Resources, pages 69–70

1. Sample answers:

I can reduce by...	I can reuse by...	I can recycle by...
- using paper on both sides - buying things that do not have a lot of packaging - bringing my own bags when shopping - drinking water from the tap instead of buying bottled water	- reusing wrapping paper and bags that gifts come in - donating things I do not want or selling them in a garage sale - making my own containers for pencils and other things from boxes or tins	- putting all paper, glass, and cans in recycling bins - composting food waste and using it for the garden - collecting rainwater to use on plants instead of tap water

2. If you use all the parts of an animal, you would end up with more useful items. You would also not have to use more resources to get all the things you made from that animal.
3. If you moved around during the year, you probably would not use all the resources in one place. Plant and animal resources would increase in number if you left them alone for a while.
4. Many people think humans are the most important things in the world and that their needs come above all other concerns.

Forms of Energy, pages 71–72

1. a) motion
   b) motion
   c) chemical
   d) thermal
   e) electrical
2. They are renewable because they are always available. They will never be used up.
3. They are non-renewable because they can be used up. They take millions of years to form.
4. Wind could be important in places where the wind blows all the time or most of the time. But wind could not be used in places where there is not a lot of wind.
5. Answers might include points such as the following: There are many types of fossil fuels in the world right now. Fossil fuels are often found in large areas. So when you dig a mine to get coal, there is a lot of coal to take out.

Word Stretch: Sample answer: *Biology* is the study of life. *Geography* is the study of land. A *hydroplane* is a type of boat that moves very fast over the surface of the water.

Fossil Fuels, pages 73–74

1. Sample answer: plants in swamps died → plants sank to the bottom of the swamp → plants formed peat → peat was covered by materials that turned into rock → more rock was formed → rock pressed down and squeezed the water out of the peat → peat turned into natural gas, oil, or coal
2. Sample answer: It would be easier to drill on land because the land does not move. You could put equipment on land and it would be safe. On the ocean, you would have to build something like a raft to put equipment on. The raft would move around, which would be dangerous. A drill in the ocean has to go all the way to the bottom before it hits ground.
3. Natural gas can be dangerous because it burns easily. If gas had no odor, you might not know when there was a gas leak. You might accidentally start a fire or cause an explosion. The added odor allows you to smell a gas leak and gives you a chance to leave the building. You could then call someone to fix the leak before a fire or explosion happens.

Word Stretch *Petrify* means to turn wood or other organic materials into rock. *Petroglyph* refers to a carving, drawing, or painting made on rock long ago.

How We Use Energy, pages 75–76

1. Sample answers: Machines are used to make item and to perform tasks. All machines need energy to work. Many items such as cars and toys are made by machines in production plants. Machines are used to make natural resources into products such as copper and wood. Machines extract fossil fuels from the ground. They are also used to grow food on farms and to cut down forests. Because machines are used to do so many things, industries use a lot of energy.
2. People who use propane or wood might live away from towns and cities. They might not be able to get electricity or natural gas where they live. Some people might not want to use fossil fuels, so they would use wood instead.
3. Today, people have more appliances in their homes. People also have more electronic devices, such as televisions and CD players. Most homes have computers now, which was not the case 20 years ago.
4. Sample answer: The kitchen because of appliances that use energy.

How Does Energy Work? pages 77–78

1. Designs will vary. Ensure student designs follow the guidelines.

Energy Vocabulary, page 80

1. a) dump; It does not conserve resources.
   b) biomass; It is a renewable energy source.
   c) harvested; It is not a form of energy.
   d) fossil fuels; It is a non-renewable energy source.
2. a) renewable
   b) extracted
   c) conservation
   d) petroleum
   e) transformation
3. Sample answer:
   a) can be replaced by nature or through good management practices

b) pulled out, often with great force or effort
c) the preservation and protection of something; managing resources wisely
d) a dark oil brought up from under Earth's surface; a fossil fuel; also called crude oil
e) changing in form or shape

Conserving Energy, pages 81–83

1. Look for arguments supported by facts.
2. Natural gas, because it is a non-renewable resource so it will run out over time. Hydropower is energy that comes from using water, and water is a renewable resource.
3. Sample answer: Solar power can only work where there is a lot of sunlight. Many places do not get enough sunlight. Solar power can only make energy during the day. We need energy all day and night. The energy made during the day may not be enough for the night too.
4. Sample answers:
   b) Turn out the lights when you leave your bedroom.
   c) Let your hair dry in the air instead.
   d) Do not run the water all the time while brushing.
   e) Only wash clothes when you have a full load. Use cold water.
   f) Take a shower instead of a bath.
   g) Buy an energy-efficient television. Turn the television off when you leave the room.
   h) Turn the computer off when you are not using it. Use a laptop instead of a desktop computer.
   i) Do not use the heat cycle to dry the dishes. Open the dishwasher and let the dishes air dry.
   j) Walk, ride a bike, or take a bus to school.

The Impact of Resource and Energy Use, pages 84–85

1. Sample answers:
   a) support; There will be jobs building the dam and running the plant.
   b) oppose; The dam would have negative affects on the plants and animals in the area.
   c) support; The town needs money for things such as schools, hospitals, and building roads.
   d) support; They may think local power costs less.
   e) oppose; the number of fish would decrease and the fish might disappear

Take a Point of View, page 86

Answers will vary.

What Does a Marine Biologist Do? pages 89–90

1. Marine animals are animals that live in the ocean.
2. Yes. The article says there are thousands of marine plants and animals, so many marine biologists choose to study just one thing.
3. Some marine biologists work on boats to study whales that come to the surface, and some work in laboratories to observe fish in large water tanks, or look at tiny sea creatures under a microscope.
4. Example: Because scuba divers and the people in the submarine have to be able to breathe air, so they cannot stay down for a very long time.
5. It has a lot of lights to help scientists see things in the deep water. It has claws to help it pick things up underwater.
6. Marine biologists share information by writing scientific reports.

What Does a Carpenter Do? pages 91–92

1. Nails, screws, and glue are materials that carpenters use to join together pieces of wood.
2. The author provided these examples to help readers understand what power tools are.
3. The energy that hand tools need to do work comes from the carpenter's muscles.
4. Building a bridge: construction carpenter. Replacing a home's old staircase: residential carpenter
5. A residence is a home, a place where people live.
6. Sample answers:
   Similar: To put together a bookshelf, you join together pieces of wood, just like a furniture maker does.
   Different: A furniture maker cuts wood. You do not need to cut wood when you put together a bookcase from a store; the pieces are already the right size and shape. (Students might also mention that a furniture maker sands and stains the wood, which is not required when putting together a bookshelf from a store.)

The Computer Revolution, pages 93–94

1. Answers will vary.
2. Sample answers: to do research for projects, do homework, email friends and relatives, play computer games, buy things from online stores, listen to music, watch videos and movies, look at photographs, create presentations
3. Sample answer: First you have to think of an idea, but most of the hard work is in building it and making it work.
4. Sample answer: Smaller computers take up less space, so you can fit them anywhere or easily carry them with you when you go somewhere.

Greetings from Kentucky

Greetings from Kentucky

A Post Card Tour, 1900-1950

Wade Hall

THE UNIVERSITY PRESS OF KENTUCKY

Scholarly publisher for the Commonwealth,
serving Bellarmine College, Berea College, Centre
College of Kentucky, Eastern Kentucky University,
The Filson Club, Georgetown College, Kentucky
Historical Society, Kentucky State University,
Morehead State University, Murray State University,
Northern Kentucky University, Transylvania University,
University of Kentucky, University of Louisville,
and Western Kentucky University.

Editorial and Sales Offices: Lexington, Kentucky 40508-4008

Library of Congress Cataloging-in-Publication Data

Hall, Wade H.
Greetings from Kentucky : a post card tour , 1900-1950 / Wade Hall.
p. cm.
Includes index.
ISBN 0-8131-1887-5
1. Kentucky—Pictorial works. 2. Postcards—Kentucky. I. Title.
F452.H35 1994
976.9' 04—dc20 94-11165

This book is printed on acid-free recycled paper meeting
the requirements of the American National Standard
for Permanence of Paper for Printed Library Materials.

For
the thousands of Kentuckians
whom I have taught for more than 30 years:
You have taught me
to love the vital history, the rich culture,
and the awesome natural beauty
of this first flower of the American West

Contents

Introduction

I don't remember the first time I ever *received* a picture post card, but the first time I ever *sent* one was from Heidelberg, Germany, in the mid-1950s, when I was in the U.S. Army. I had just arrived from the States, and I wanted my family to *see* what Germany looked like. I went to the Post Exchange and selected a bird's-eye view of the city taken from the top of a nearby mountain. In the weeks and months that followed, I mailed dozens of picture post cards back home to friends and relatives. I was able to show my distant readers, none of whom had ever been to Europe, what I was seeing as I traveled around Germany, France, Switzerland, Austria, Belgium, Luxembourg, Holland, and England. It was a pattern of communication that had been set in the United States as early as 1893 with post card views of the World's Columbian Exposition in Chicago as the nation celebrated the four hundredth anniversary of the European discovery of the New World.

Like wildfire, the post card fad spread, and before the turn of the new century, many towns and cities throughout the nation had their main streets, churches and schools, scenic views and monuments and famous citizens depicted on post cards. They were not only inexpensive and convenient but beautiful forms of democratic art that anyone could afford. Soon people began to form post card clubs and collect cards from all over the country, placing them carefully in attractive albums that enjoyed a place of honor in middle-class parlors next to the family Bible. This buying and sending and collecting craze continued until after World War I, when their popularity abated somewhat as the nation's tastes in popular art became more sophisticated and other forms of personal communication began to compete. Moreover, the artistic quality of the post card images had declined because the trade in cards produced by skilled German printers had been stopped by the war.

Nevertheless, the picture post card had become a fixture in American life. Even today, despite the omnipresence of the telephone and the fax machine, few people leave home for more than a couple of days without mailing back post card views and comments on their trip. It is still a handy and effective way of saying, "Arrived safely. Here is where I am. Wish you were here." This colorful record has a dimension lacking in a letter or the plain vanilla government postal card. Indeed, since the 1970s there has been a resurgence of interest in collecting vintage as well as contemporary cards. Thousands of people belong again to post card clubs and tens of thousands attend post card shows each year. These people call themselves deltiologists, a fancy word for one who sends, receives, collects, and studies post cards.

Although there is a great deal of overlapping, deltiologists usually divide post card history into seven periods. The Pioneer Period ran from its beginnings in Europe in the 1870s to 1898, when Congress authorized "Private Mailing Cards" that carried a mailing rate reduced from two cents to one cent, the same as the government issue cards, which had been available since 1873. It was also in 1898 that the mailing of post cards received another boost when Congress authorized Rural Free Delivery, which made sending and receiving all types of mail easy and inexpensive for the majority of Americans who still lived in rural areas. "Mail riders," as country people often called them, made front-yard deliveries and pick-ups on horseback and buggy and later by automobile.

This Private Mailing Card Period (1898-1901) began the mania for post card sending and collecting. Post card clubs and publications sprouted all over the land. The Undivided Back Period (1901-07) permitted only "Post Card" to be printed on the address side. No personal message was allowed, except whatever the sender could squeeze in on or around the picture. The Divided Back Period (1907-15) allowed a personal greeting on the left side of a vertical line, with the address on the right side. By then, hardly anyone left home without promising to mail back a chain of cards that chronicled the traveler's journey. Cards were readily available almost anywhere, in such places as train stations, drug stores, hotels, book and stationery shops, and souvenir stands and could be mailed at convenient mail drops and even on board trains at Railroad Post Offices.

The White Border Period (1916-30) was ushered in by the world war, when almost all post cards were produced by domestic manufacturers. They were printed with white borders that were supposed to save ink. For many collectors this period signaled the end of collectible post cards. The sixth or Linen Period (1930-45) produced cards on textured paper using often garish inks that sometimes fade. Cards during this period were frequently based on black and white photographs that had been reworked by artists, then painted in watercolors before printing. The process produced an often stylized, surreal image that collectors are now beginning to value. Post cards of the final or Chrome Period (since 1945) are usually glossy color copies of color photographs. During this period advances in color photography have made it possible to produce cards with sharp, color-correct images made from transparencies. All periods of post cards are now collected and treasured for their artistic and historical values, but most collectors are still partial to those that portray eras rapidly vanishing from human memory.

Collectors are also increasingly intrigued by the messages that these cards carried. Because of the cramped writing space, especially before 1907, there developed a post card shorthand made up of inventive abbreviations: "Arr OK. Saw bro Seth at rr stat. Go to ss and ch Sun." Collectors are also attracted by photograph cards, or Real Photos, made possible in 1902 when the Eastman Kodak Company introduced a camera and post card size paper on which photographs could be printed directly from negatives. This invention made it possible for almost anyone to have personalized cards featuring his or her own likeness.

From the beginning, of course, post card subjects reflected the broad tastes and interests of the American people, from comic cards with ethnic barbs directed at the Irish or Scots or Indians or blacks or hillbillies to those that celebrated religious holidays and holy images. Post cards were designed for every special day on the calendar, from New Year's Day to St. Patrick's Day to Halloween to Groundhog Day. It has been estimated that as many as 10,000 different Santa Claus cards have been issued. There were also brightly embossed cards designed by such talented artists as Ellen Clapsaddle, Frances Brundage, and H.B. Griggs. Such special events as fairs, chautauquas, political conventions and expositions were promoted. Famous people, historical and contemporary, were honored with cards. There were novelty cards that talked, sang, or popped up or were decorated with ribbons, real hair, and dried flowers. Women with such common names as Martha or Sarah or Adelaide could buy cards with their names embossed on them. Current events produced many cards, often with a satirical bent. The Woman's Suffrage Movement, for example, was a popular target. A 1910 card shows a henpecked husband dressed in a maid's apron on his knees cleaning the floor, saying plaintively, "My wife's joined the Suffrage Movement (I've suffered ever since!)"

In addition, there were all-purpose generic cards that could be used to represent any place. A circa 1909 card showing a smartly dressed woman detraining with hordes of people welcoming her, reads: "They gave me a great reception at ________________________." The purchaser could fill in the blank with her destination. A bevy of beautiful girls could serve as "the Girls of Bowling Green" or "the Girls of

Paintsville." Other generic cards showed identical rural scenes and could read variously: "Enjoying the beautiful scenery at Waddy"—or Calhoun or Summer Shade or Cutshin or Monkeys Eyebrow.

Among this huge variety, however, it was the view card showing actual places that dominated the industry from the start. Cards showing main streets, important buildings, hotels, restaurants, and tourist attractions could show the folks at home what you were seeing. View cards of Kentucky became instant bestsellers with Kentuckians as well as visitors. State pride was still running high in 1893, the year after Kentuckians celebrated their centennial as the fifteenth state. The state was, therefore, ready turf for the introduction of post cards featuring Kentucky images. Although some cards printed before 1900 are extant, it was not until early in the twentieth century that travelers could find views of just about any place in the state, from Greenup to Guthrie, from Pikeville to Paducah. In October of 1906 Ada in Louisville sent Edith in Somerset a view of Fourth Avenue and exclaimed: "On this street is where most of the big stores are. You can always find pretty things here."

Bird's-eye cards of Kentucky cities and towns showed high-view vistas of cityscapes. Close-up views of streets were also very popular, and through the years they show not only the architectural changes in homes and commercial buildings but also the evolution of transportation, from wagons, buggies, and carriages to trolleys, streetcars, and finally automobiles and buses. Moreover, post cards chronicle the wider progress of transportation in Kentucky from steamboats to the air age. The coming of the affordable automobile to Kentucky in the 1920s gave a burst of popularity to post cards. Motorists could travel at their own convenience from place to place within the state and from Kentucky to other states. They could stay at the older hotels or choose the newer tourist homes and cottages and motels. Sometimes the traveler would put an X by a room or a cottage, explaining, "This is where we slept last night." Furthermore, post cards provide us with a visual history of Kentucky's roadside architecture—a service station near Covington, a motel south of Somerset, a Wigwam Village near Cave City, a reptile zoo near Park City, and numerous bridges spanning Kentucky's waterways.

Post cards featuring such public places as courthouses, churches, post offices, train depots, fire stations—even cemeteries and penal institutions—became very popular. Cards often provide us with documentation of buildings and institutions that no longer exist.

Where are Hamilton College in Lexington, Warren Baptist Academy in Smiths Grove, Bethel Female Academy in Hopkinsville, Science Hill Academy in Shelbyville, Jessamine Institute in Nicholasville, Princeton Collegiate Institute, or Warren Memorial Presbyterian Church that used to stand in downtown Louisville? They are all gone with the years, but on post cards they left images as bright as today.

Even some illegal products and activities are celebrated on Kentucky's post cards. Moonshine stills graced many a card sent from Kentucky around the globe and unfortunately helped perpetuate Kentucky's image as a backward, scofflaw state. In 1907 T.P. Curry & Son in Danville published a "Souvenir Letter of Kentucky Hemp Fields," which showed the now dastardly marijuana plant being grown, cut, spread, shocked, and broken—all parts of the process of making hemp into rope, of course.

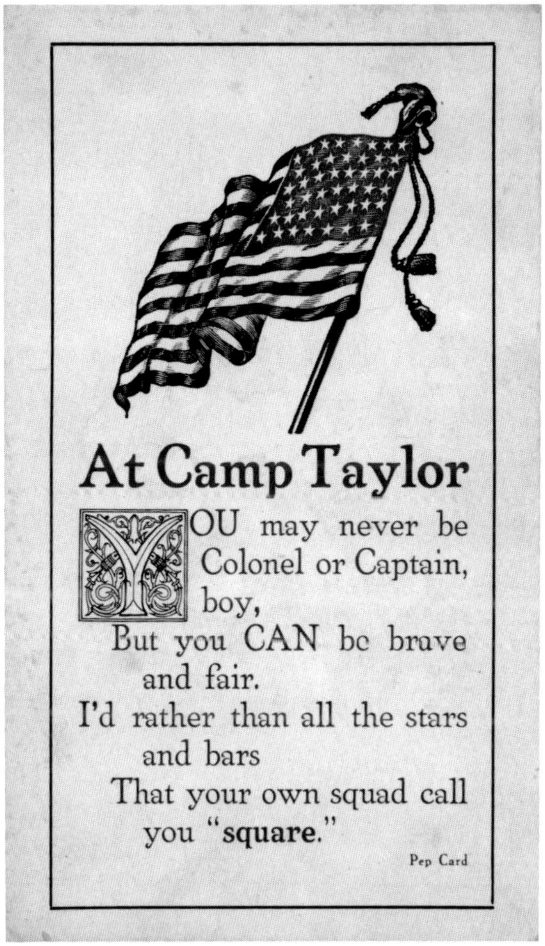

There is nothing like a grand tragedy to bring out the cameras and, quickly following, post card views that have commemorated Kentucky's natural and manmade disasters: a devastating flood in Louisville, a powerful tornado in Bowling Green, an automobile accident. Brave firefighters and selfless soldiers are depicted on many cards as heroes in time of distress. Kentucky's role in our nation's wars is reflected on cards of soldiers and scenes at Camp Taylor and Fort Knox and Fort Campbell, stretching, on historical cards, all the way back to the American Revolution and the Civil War. Real Photo cards allowed young men to pretend that they were wild and woolly cowboys playing cards in a saloon—all within the safe walls of a photographer's studio in Lexington or Louisville. Other Real Photo cards show individuals and families in exotic studio settings or in front of their homes and barns, sometimes with a new wagon and horse in the foreground.

Real and imagined historic sites have been favorites with Kentuckians and visitors alike: the Wilderness Road leading from Virginia into Kentucky; the Fort Harrod and Boonesboro reconstructions; Federal Hill, or "My Old Kentucky Home," in Bardstown; and views of "Kentucky's First Cabin" or "Boone's First Home in Kentucky." Also featured on numerous post cards are the homes of such state luminaries as John Hunt Morgan of Lexington, vice-president Alben Barkley in Paducah, Isaac Shelby near Danville, Simon Bolivar Buckner near Munfordville, and, more recently, Loretta Lynn in Butcher Hollow. One card pictures a house near Lancaster and states unequivocally that here is the birthplace of Harriet Beecher Stowe's *Uncle Tom's Cabin*—"where the story was written."

Kentucky's rich religious heritage is reflected on cards showing the Cane Ridge Meeting House in Bourbon County, where the Christian Church originated; the Shaker colonies at Pleasant Hill and South Union; the Southern Baptist and Presbyterian theological seminaries in

Louisville; and the Trappist Abbey of Gethsemani near Bardstown. Needless to say, post card views of local Baptist, Methodist, Presbyterian, Catholic, and Episcopal churches could be had from Morgantown to Morganfield, from Falmouth to Fulton.

Politics, a major Kentucky occupation and preoccupation, is recorded on post cards honoring officeholders who have achieved the stature of statesmen, usually a number of years after their deaths. Sometimes candidates mailed post card pictures of themselves to voters and stated their platforms in narrow planks. Two native sons who presided over the fates of the Union and the Confederacy were popular subjects, with Abraham Lincoln, who had received but a handful of Kentucky's votes in the presidential election of 1860, easily winning over Jefferson Davis in the post card sweepstakes. During the centenary of Lincoln's birth in 1909, thousands of cards featuring his humble birthplace near Hodgenville were circulated, many of them by Kentuckians. On the other hand, the Confederacy easily won the monument war, with dozens of post cards depicting public statues honoring the fallen heroes of the Lost Cause.

Other famous Kentucky natives or adoptees graced many a post card, from Daniel Boone, Henry Clay, and Stephen Collins Foster to Floyd Collins, who was fatally trapped in Sand Cave in 1925, and Jean Thomas, the folksinger known as the "Traipsin' Woman" of Ashland. More Kentuckians immortalized on the 3 1/2" x 5 1/2" cards include Richard M. Johnson, vice-president of the United States and reputed slayer of Chief Tecumseh; Zachary Taylor, twelfth president of the United States; and John Fitch, the alleged inventor of the steamboat, who committed suicide in Bardstown in 1798. Last, and certainly not least, are the cards that celebrate the larger-than-human icons, Man O' War and Secretariat.

Kentuckians at play are pictured on post cards ranging from the era of the popular mineral resorts, or spas, when there were more than a hundred such watering places throughout Kentucky, down to the basketball glory days of the state's colleges and universities. Churchill Downs, the Red Mile, Keeneland, Latonia Race Track, and other sites of the sport of kings—made possible, it is said, by the rich limestone-nourished bluegrass that in turn nourished world-renowned racehorses—occupied thousands of post cards. Meanwhile, below ground other revelers, perhaps more sensibly, explored caves occurring in that same limestone.

Lest we forget that Kentucky is not only a democratic state but a capitalistic one, there are post cards to remind us that showcasing and promoting products and services have always been prime missions of the little card. Merchants, in particular, have thus advertised their wares cheaply and effectively. In the 1930s Wallerstein's, a men's clothier in

Paducah, boasted by card that here was where Irvin S. Cobb, the famous author/actor and native of their fair city, had "bought his first pair of short pants, and later, his first pair of long ones." A few years later, in another part of the state, a post card pictures Sanders Court & Cafe near Corbin, with thirty-two rooms and thirty-two baths. Its owner, just plain Harland Sanders before he got promoted to colonel, boasted that he was "serving excellent food" without mentioning his fried chicken or secret herbs and spices.

The documentary photographer Walker Evans once wrote in an article in *Fortune* magazine that post cards are "some of the truest visual records ever made of any period." That assertion, however, is an inflated claim, and a word of caution is in order when using post card images or printed statements as documentary evidence. Post cards usually tell the truth, but they can also tell half-truths and occasional lies. Post card images, for example, may be carefully contrived and manipulated to present a preconceived view of a person or a place or an issue. Business owners who wanted their shops or tourist cabins or eateries spruced up by the printer's artists would have them apply a new coat of paint or remove an unsightly building or tree or place a new convertible at the curb of a drive-in restaurant. Furthermore, suppositions and theories are sometimes given as facts. A card featuring a desk from Federal Hill in Bardstown states bluntly that it is the desk "where Stephen C. Foster penned his immortal song 'My Old Kentucky Home' in 1852." Of the daredevil cave explorer and self-seeking entrepreneur Floyd Collins, a card gushes this saccharine sentiment: "He lived for an ideal—in search of earthly beauty. This he found in his discovery of Crystal Cave. He died for an ideal—the ideal of service before self." Finally, during the periods of the idealized Christy Girl and the Gibson Girl and the days of much lace and big hats, the post card women were always beautiful—except, of course, in the case of comic cards ridiculing Old Maids, which, in fact, were usually men dressed as women.

Unfortunately, for most of post card history Kentucky has been, at least for visitors, a state of stereotypes: the goateed colonel holding a mint julep, the cretin-like rustic making moonshine or slouching on the sagging

porch of a ramshackle cabin, the little black boy with exaggerated features playing hooky at the fishpond. Furthermore, Kentucky's literary reputation was hardly enhanced by the reams of bad verse that sincerely sought to extoll the wonders and glories of Kentucky's land, people, and history. Probably the best known—and the worst written— is James H. Mulligan's "In Kentucky," where "moonlight falls the softest, . . . home fires burn the brightest, . . . bluegrass waves the bluest, . . . moonshine is the clearest," and, to add a little realism, "taxes are the highest" and "politics—the damndest."

Such bad writing in both poetry and prose gave a pseudo-literary dimension to thousands of post cards. The glories of Kentucky are hailed in this bloated prose by Bruce Barton in his "Tribute to Kentucky": "Kentucky's sons and daughters know no sweeter place to live. Her guests can find no friendlier place to visit than Kentucky, gracious daughter of the Old Dominion." In "After a Visit to Old Kentucky" an anonymous versemaker testifies in rustic dialect to the visitor's longing to return to the hospitality, the friendliness, the wonders of the state, summing it up thusly: "I be'n in ole Kentucky, / An' I wan' o' go ag'in." Another anonymous poetaster asserts that he wouldn't take the Czar's kingdom "for one corner of old Kaintuck." Of course, there is always a wag in the woods who shoots his poisoned arrow at the high-flying balloon to bring it back to earth. Such a satirist was the anonymous author of "In Far-Famed Old Kentucky," a parody of Mulligan's poem. In the revised version, Kentucky is "Where the blood it flows like water, and the bullets fly like hail, / Where every pistol has a pocket, and every coat has a tail, / Where they always hang the jury, but they never hang the man, / Where you call a man a liar, then go home if you can." But, of course, such trash was for the titillation and economic exploitation of outlanders who were just passing through and wanted their prejudices confirmed. Closer to the truth, naturally, is this post card verse of ultimate chauvinism, which John A. Logan called modestly "God Lives in Kentucky": "It is just as clear as can be / That God loves and freely gives / To the other States His blessings; / But Kentucky's where he lives."

Less bombastic and much more credible were the

A KENTUCKY WELCOME

BY G. ALLISON HOLLAND.

From Kentucky's hills and valleys, from the grassy dells and plain,
Hear the notes of joyous welcome she extends,
From her wealth of bud and blossom, growing in the sun and rain,
You'll find all that hospitality commends,
You'll catch the scent of lilacs and of violets and mint,
When the reddening sky foretells the coming night,
And your heart beats fast and faster in the gloaming and the glint,
As we holler to you: ' Stranger! stop and light.'

Old Kentucky may be slower than her neighbors in some ways,
But yields no point to any other clime
When it comes to cordial greetings—and you'll find it as we say,
That heart is in the right place all the time.
True, there is the juicy julep, and the touching of the glass,
And the flashing of the bird wings in their flight,
But Kentucky loves to welcome all her good friends as they pass
With a hearty "Howdy! stranger, stop and light."

simple messages and verses penned (or more often penciled) by the millions of people who wrote their own words on cards. These messages were often simple greetings to friends and family to indicate personal or family conditions or a safe arrival: "Having a swell time. Good trip. Wonderful weather." In July of 1942 a Louisville war factory worker wrote to her mother in Hardinsburg that she had finished her shift and had to hurry and "write to my soldier & wash my hair." In August of 1949 a man who had recently arrived in Louisville wrote to his lady friend in Fort Worth this iconoclastic rhyme: "The trip was fine / the weather is hell / the sun won't shine / it really is swell— / for fish."

As Kentuckians took to the roads in large numbers in the 1920s and 1930s, post cards were an easy way for travelers to assure the homefolks by picture and word that they were progressing with all deliberate speed or had arrived safely. In September of 1956 a woman on her way to "our winter home" wrote from Yeary's Tourist Court in Corbin to a friend in Cincinnati, thanking her for hospitality, and adding: "When we get settled in Fla., you must stop with us." In August 1928 a woman wrote from Winchester to a male friend in Latonia, somewhat cryptically: "We are getting a big thrill out of traveling by ourselves. We bought a newspaper and the porter brushed us off." Cards were sometimes used to report car trouble and delays. A card written from Lexington in 1932 by Pearl to a friend in Michigan stated: "Had a little bad luck with car today but all set now. Will stay in Lexington tonight." In May of 1909 a man in Louisville wrote his sister in Henderson: "Pa arrived on time. Safe & sound. Have not had time to examine all of his bundles, but Sis says the cake is fine."

Salesmen found post cards an invaluable keep-in-touch aid as they traveled around the state and country. In February of 1910 a salesman in Bowling Green wrote his girlfriend in Louisville: "Will finish this town Tuesday. We leave for Princeton next." A month later he wrote from Henderson: "Will finish here late tomorrow. We then go to Owensboro." Often the messages were quick announcements of schedule changes. In March of 1912, Graham in Hodgenville wrote Mae in Leitchfield: "I cannot come down Easter on account of train doesn't run & couldn't get back to work."

On their post cards Kentuckians have written about all the things that interest them, from movies, food, and basketball to politics, horses, and dating the opposite sex—frequently without concern for the post card's lack of privacy. A student at Georgetown College wrote to her friend Minnie in Louisville from the reputedly strict Baptist college on February 1, 1938: "Who says they don't dance at Georgetown? Woo! Woo! I have found <u>him</u> already. Also have 2 other suckers on a string. Details later." One can only hope that she entrusted the intimate "details" to the security of a sealed letter. It might also have been more decorous had a woman in Chilesburg used a letter to write her nephew in Latonia this disgusting report in July of 1941: "Mae and I got home OK last night. I held that 'rare' bull I ate down till I got home and up it came. It didn't waste for the dog ate it that time." Well, maybe that message cured some nosey mail carrier of reading other people's cards.

Occasionally the message is so warped one assumes the writer simply made a careless scribal error that went uncorrected. How else can you explain this card mailed from Louisville by a man to a woman in Henderson: "Am having a time of your life. Will be home tonight." And a 1907 view of the State Prison in Frankfort has this revealing question: "Do you remember being here?" Reading such messages on other people's post cards fifty or a hundred years later may be a harmless if somewhat puzzling pastime. Indeed, when the haste of composition and the telegraphic style demanded by post cards are mixed with a penchant for misspelling, bad penmanship, and sloppy grammar, it is small wonder that messages are often hard to decipher. One can sympathize with the young Princeton student who wrote a friend in Louisville in 1912: "Had a post card from your aunt & couldn't make out a single word." Still, the most welcome message is as simple and satisfying as this card from a woman in Franklin to a friend in Webster: "Your card did me a world of good to know you had not forgotten me." Furthermore, as was usually the case, these friends had the satisfaction of knowing that the pictures on the cards they exchanged were selected for each other.

Like a rummage through Grandmother's trunk, these cards show us who we Kentuckians were for almost a century, warts and all. At last, the humble post card has become acclaimed as a work of democratic art and as a way to document the past. Moreover, the transportation and communication revolutions of our time have not made it obsolete. Picture post cards are as varied and available as ever. On a recent trip to Milwaukee to see a folk art exhibition, I bought a post card showing a wood carving by the late Kentucky artist Edgar Tolson and mailed it to a friend in Harrodsburg. "Here's a little bit of Kentucky way up here," I wrote, and proved it with a picture. Now, in these pages you will see the panorama that was Kentucky for the first half of the twentieth century. This is, indeed, the way we were—from a view of Lexington's Main Street in 1908 to a drive-in restaurant near Shively in 1950. Travel Kentucky from A to Z. Look and enjoy.

—Wade Hall

A is for . . .

Advertising

These promotional cards were used by a clothing store in Frankfort, a craft shop at Berea College, a bank in Lexington, and a popular Kentucky whiskey that employed a racial stereotype to sell its product.

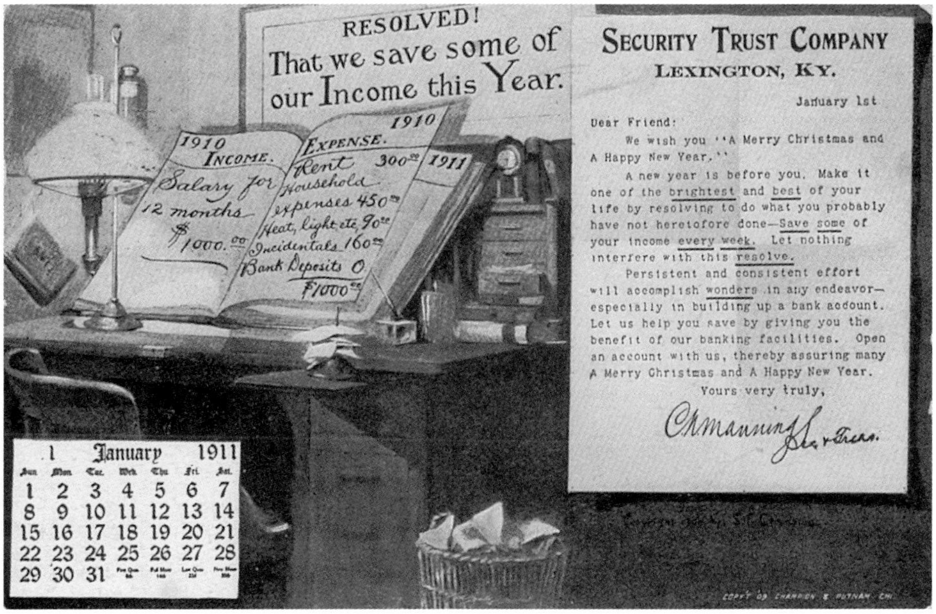

SNOOPY
MAMMY
SCOTTY
DAVID DUCK
MARIANNE
COCKY LOCKY
JACK
"Cuddle Toys"
FROM THE NEEDLECRAFT OF
BEREA COLLEGE STUDENT INDUSTRIES
BEREA, KENTUCKY
8A-H744

GREEN RIVER
WHISKEY
WITHOUT
A
HEADACHE
"SHE WAS BRED IN OLD KENTUCKY"

African American

Blacks have been an integral part of the Kentucky experience for over two hundred years, during which time they have worked and played and, sadly, been caricatured and stereotyped.

A one-time popular gathering place for African Americans in Louisville.

Ashland

The largest city in Eastern Kentucky was home to one Kentucky governor, Simeon Willis (1943-47), and two Supreme Court justices, Fred Vinson and Stanley Reed. Ashland is the center of one of the most heavily industrialized regions in the state.

B is for . . .

Barbourville

Situated on the Cumberland River, the seat of Knox County is the home of Union College.

Bardstown

The seat of Nelson County, Bardstown is a center of tourism and distilling and the site of Federal Hill, "My Old Kentucky Home."

Alben W. Barkley

The Kentucky senator and vice-president of the United States (1949-53) was a native of Graves County.

Basketball

Miss Augusta Kiefer, a guard on the 1918 championship girls' basketball team at Barret-Manual Training High School in Henderson, exemplifies Kentuckians' long-standing devotion to the sport.

Bellevue

This Ohio River town in Campbell County was the birthplace of painter-writer-naturalist Harlan Hubbard.

Berea

The Madison County town was founded in the 1850s by abolitionist preacher John Gregg Fee, who also established the interracial school that became Berea College.

Bloomfield

The Nelson County town is site of the double grave of Jereboam O. Beauchamp and his wife, Ann. Beauchamp's 1825 murder of a former Kentucky attorney general who had allegedly seduced Ann resulted in several novels.

Bluegrass

In certain lights, this dark green grass *(Poa pratensis)* produces a seed that appears blue to all but the most iconoclastic botanist.

Daniel Boone

The Pennsylvania-born explorer and pioneer symbolizes the early West.

THE BOONE MONUMENT. FRANKFORT. KY.

Bourbon

This Kentucky-bred whiskey is made from a fermented mash of corn, wheat, rye, and barley, plus yeast and limestone water, and is aged in charred oak barrels.

FAMOUS OLD TAYLOR DISTILLERY

Bowling Green

The largest city in southern Kentucky was the short-lived Confederate capital of the state. It is now the home of Western Kentucky University.

Bridges

They span rivers and creeks throughout Kentucky, making possible rapid transportation by foot, horse, wagon, train, and automobile. The most famous is the Roebling Suspension Bridge over the Ohio River between Covington and Cincinnati, which opened in 1867.

Bridges

BRIDGE OVER DIX RIVER NEAR LANCASTER, KY.

Steamer Jewell at the L. & N. Bridge, Henderson, Ky.

2636 HIGH BRIDGE KENTUCKY

Panhandle Bridge, Louisville. Ky.

OHIO RIVER BRIDGE CONNECTING MADISON, INDIANA AND TRIMBLE COUNTY, KENTUCKY
BEDFORD IS THE COUNTY SEAT OF TRIMBLE COUNTY, KENTUCKY

Old Bridge over Beech Fork River, Bardstown Ky.

View of Brooksville, Ky.

Brooksville

The seat of Bracken County was once known as Woodwards Crossroads.

Simon Bolivar Buckner

Governor of Kentucky (1887-91) and a Confederate general, Buckner was a native of Hart County.

GLEN LILY, HOME OF GENERAL BUCKNER, HART COUNTY, KENTUCKY

Main Street Looking West, Burgin, Ky.

Burgin

This Mercer County town is at the head of Cane Run.

Burgoo

A stew of uncertain ancestry, burgoo is often made in large vats for political meetings, family reunions, and Kentucky Colonel gatherings. Its ingredients range from garden sass to forest varmints.

Burnside

First called Camp Burnside for Union General Ambrose Burnside, this Pulaski County town was located on the Cumberland River until 1950, when the old town was flooded by the impoundment that created Lake Cumberland and a new town was built on higher ground. The old town was fondly remembered by writer Harriette Simpson Arnow as her birthplace.

C is for . . .

Campbellsville
The seat of Taylor County was invaded by both sides during the Civil War, losing its courthouse to a Confederate incendiary.

Carrollton
First called Port William, the seat of Carroll County is home to one of Kentucky's popular state parks.

Catlettsburg

The seat of Boyd County, where the Ohio and Big Sandy rivers meet, grew up around Horatio Catlett's tavern and once had twenty-one saloons on Front Street.

Caves

Kentucky has almost 800 miles of surveyed passages, including the huge system known as Mammoth Cave.

Cemeteries

They were popular post card subjects, including one at tiny Foster in Bracken County that apparently had the bulk of its population in the cemetery, according to the message on this 1923 card: "Dont think this place is dead because I'm sending you this picture, but it's so near it that this is the only card I can find. (Ha! Ha!)"

Odd Fellows' Cemetery, Foster, Ky.

Louisville, Ky., in Cave Hill Cemetery, Driveways and Chapel.

WOOLDRIDGE MONUMENTS ERECTED 1894 IN CEMETERY, MAYFIELD, KY. A-12824

Churches

Kentucky has representatives of most religious groups in the world, with Baptists the most numerous.

Highland Baptist Church, 1501 Cherokee Road, Rev. L. W. Doolan, Pastor

Old Mud Meeting House, in Mercer County, near Harrodsburg, Ky. Erected 1800.

Presbyterian Church, Bloomfield, Ky.

FAIRVIEW CHURCH, HOPKINSVILLE, KY.
BEQUEATHED BY JEFFERSON DAVIS, PRESIDENT
OF THE CONFEDERATE STATES OF AMERICA.
5573

BAPTIST CHURCH
HARDINSBURG KY

St. Martin's Church,
Louisville, Ky.
FERDINAND TONINI
FAY-MU

Methodist Church, Ghent, Ky.

Church of the Messiah (Unitarian), 901 Fourth Avenue
Rev. W. H. Ramsey, Pastor

The Old Stone Meeting House, Winchester, Ky.—22

PASSIONIST FATHERS AND ST. AGNES CATHOLIC CHURCH, NEWBURG ROAD, LOUISVILLE, KY. 2
© CAUFIELD & SHOOK, LOUISVILLE

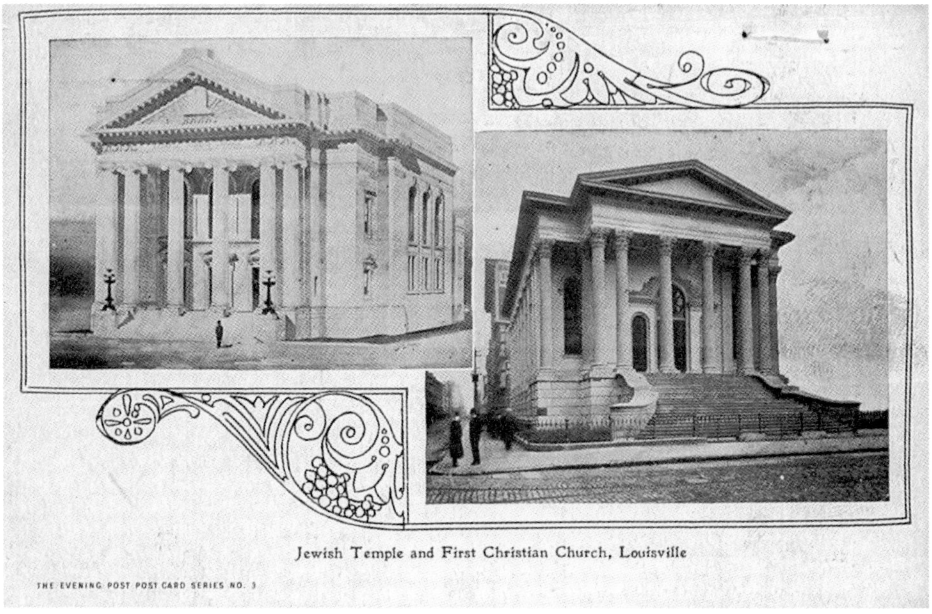
Jewish Temple and First Christian Church, Louisville
THE EVENING POST POST CARD SERIES NO. 3

St. Thomas Church,
The Founders and "Old Nazareth" 1812.

SOUTHWEST VIEW OF SHEPHERDSVILLE CAMPGROUND
SHEPHERDSVILLE, KY.
29537

Grace Episcopal Church, Louisville, Ky.

Henry Clay

The Virginia-born U.S. senator from Kentucky and Secretary of State came close to occupying the White House several times.

Coal

A major state industry—and sometimes a curse—coal exists as rich lodes concentrated in Eastern and Western Kentucky.

Hardburley Coal Tipple, near Hazard, Ky.

Coal Barges near Carrollton, Ky.

Coal Mining Camp near Middlesboro, Ky.

A Sunday School in a Kentucky Mountain Mining Camp, one of Fourteen such Sunday Schools Conducted by the Y.M.C.A. The State Y.M.C.A. Committee is extending and directing this work among the industrial workers of the mountains

The Coal House, Home of the Chamber of Commerce, Middlesboro, Ky.

Built Entirely of Kentucky Coal 111638-N

Irvin S. Cobb

The writer and actor from Paducah was creator of the Judge Priest stories.

Floyd Collins

This cave explorer's mortal entrapment in Sand Cave in 1925 and the futile attempts to rescue him became an international news event.

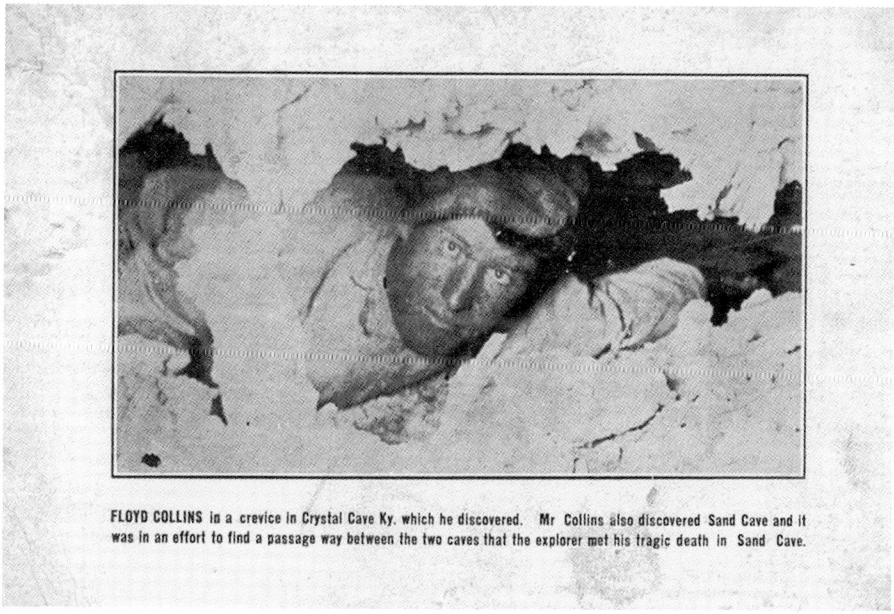

Columbia

The seat of Adair County was the scene of an 1872 bank robbery, supposedly by the Jesse James gang. The town is the home of Lindsey Wilson College, founded in 1903.

South West Corner Public Square, Columbia, Ky.

Corbin

This railroad and tourism center is in Whitley County.

Corn

An important Kentucky crop, corn is consumed by animals and humans in various forms, solid and liquid. This Lyons farmer wrote in 1908: "This is the corn I raised this year and dident have a very good crop."

Covington

Located at the confluence of the Ohio and Licking rivers across from Cincinnati, Covington is one of the two seats of Kenton County, the other being Independence.

Crescent Hill

This is one of the comfortable residential neighborhoods of Louisville.

Cumberland Falls

The sixty-eight foot falls in Whitley County is known for the occasional "moonbow" produced by mists from the falling water.

Cumberland Gap

A pass through the Cumberland Mountains in Bell County, the gap was the principal land route for pioneers coming into Kentucky in the late eighteenth century.

Cumberland Gap

CUMBERLAND GAP, A STRATEGIC CIVIL WAR POINT, NEAR PINEVILLE, KY. 88116

Cynthiana

The seat of Harrison County was named for Cynthia and Anna, two daughters of Robert Harrison, who donated the land for the town.

PIKE STREET CYNTHIANA, KY.

D is for . . .

Dams

They impound the water of Kentucky's rivers to control floods, generate electricity, and create recreational lakes.

Danville

Originally called Crow's Station, Danville is the seat of Boyle County, the home of Centre College, and the filming locale for the Civil War movie *Raintree County*. This oversize, folding card shows a panoramic view of the town.

Jefferson Davis

A Kentucky native, Davis was the only president of the Confederate States of America. He was born about a hundred miles from the Hodgenville birthplace of Abraham Lincoln, concurrent president of the United States of America.

Jefferson Davis Monument

Dawson Springs

Situated on the Tradewater River in Hopkins County, Dawson Springs was a popular health resort early in the century.

Depots

For more than a century in the heyday of the railroad, they were transportation hubs ranging from humble to palatial.

Union Station, Danville, Ky.
DANVILLE

UNION STATION, LEXINGTON, KY.—7

Disasters

They were recorded on post cards, whether caused by water, wind, mechanical failure, or human error.

149479 Fourth Avenue and theater district looking south from Chestnut Street

E is for . . .

Education

Kentucky offers it at all levels, public and private, from kindergarten through graduate and professional school. Some schools are old, some are recent, some have new names and locations, and some are only a fading photograph.

Graded School, Stanford, Lincoln County

Stenography Class—Masonic Widows' and Orphans' Home, Louisville, Ky.

Louisville Training School. Louisville, Ky.

Millersburg Military Institute, Millersburg, Ky.

Girl's High School, Louisville, Ky.

Mayfield High School Buildings, Mayfield, Ky.

High School, Augusta, Ky.

Education

11240 Loretto Academy, Loretto, Ky.

FIRESIDE INDUSTRY CABIN, HINDMAN SETTLEMENT SCHOOL, HINDMAN, KENTUCKY

BOYS DORMITORY, L. W. J. COLLEGE, COLUMBIA, KY.

Lincoln Institute of Kentucky,
Colored Normal and Industrial School,
near Simpsonville, Ky.
(Right wing of central building not yet erected.)

Transylvania University, Lexington, Ky.

ADMINISTRATION BUILDING, CUMBERLAND COLLEGE, WILLIAMSBURG, KY.
"PHOTO BY H. A. BROWNING" 868

Education

FIRST COLLEGE BUILDING ERECTED 1855
FIRST PRESIDENT'S HOUSE (FATHER FEE)
FIRST LADIES' BOARDING HALL
BEREA COLLEGE BEREA, KY.

Pikeville College and Boys Dormitory, Pikeville, Ky.
18417-N

Kentucky Female Orphan School Buildings and Campus,
Midway, Ky.

Administration Building
Kentucky Christian College, Grayson, Ky.

B. L. MIDDELTON.
DORMITORY- EASTERN KENTUCKY NORMAL SCHOOL, RICHMOND, KY.

BIRD'S-EYE VIEW OF WESTERN KENTUCKY STATE TEACHERS' COLLEGE, BOWLING GREEN, KY.
353-30

Education

Bellarmine College, Louisville, founded in 1950.

Louisville Medical College–Louisville

Presbyterian Theological Seminary, Louisville, Ky.
219852

Bryant and Stratton Business College,
Incorporated, Louisville, Kentucky.

Copyright 1905 by the Rotograph Co.
G 17047 State Normal School, Frankfort, Ky.
J. PIERCE JONES
Lock Box 134, DRAKESBORO, KY.
Many Thanks

BOWLING GREEN BUSINESS UNIVERSITY, BOWLING GREEN, KY.

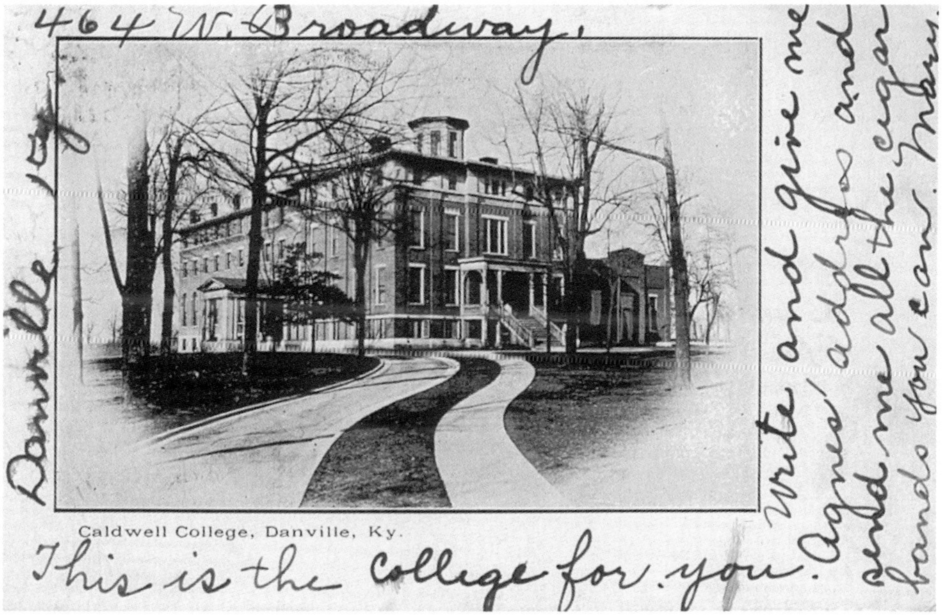

Caldwell College, Danville, Ky.

Mc Lean College, Hopkinsville, Ky.

Jessamine Institute, Nicholasville, Ky.

AUBURN SEMINARY, AUBURN, KY.

Hamilton College, Lexington, Ky.

Millersburg Female College, Millersburg, Ky.

Princeton Collegiate Institute, Princeton, Ky,

Elizabethtown

Originally named Severn's Valley for an early settler, the seat of Hardin County came to be known as "Hub City" after the convergence of three rail lines there in the 1870s and 1880s.

MAIN STREET AND DIXIE HIGHWAY SOUTH, ELIZABETHTOWN HARDIN COUNTY, KY. 111479

PUBLIC SQUARE, ELIZABETHTOWN, KY.—3

Elkhorn Creek

This waterway flows eighty-six miles across Fayette, Scott, Woodford, and Franklin counties before emptying into the Kentucky River. It was immortalized in art by Paul Sawyier and Robert Burns Wilson.

Elkton

The seat of Todd County was settled in 1817 at the nearby Elk Fork of Red River, and was named for the herds that once roamed the area

Elkton Hotel, Elkton, Ky.

Eminence

The Henry County town was reportedly given its name for being the highest point on the Louisville-Lexington railroad.

Northside of Broadway, Eminence, Ky.

F is for . . .

Farming

Most Kentuckians made their living by farming until the middle of the twentieth century, though of course not all farmers were this fetching.

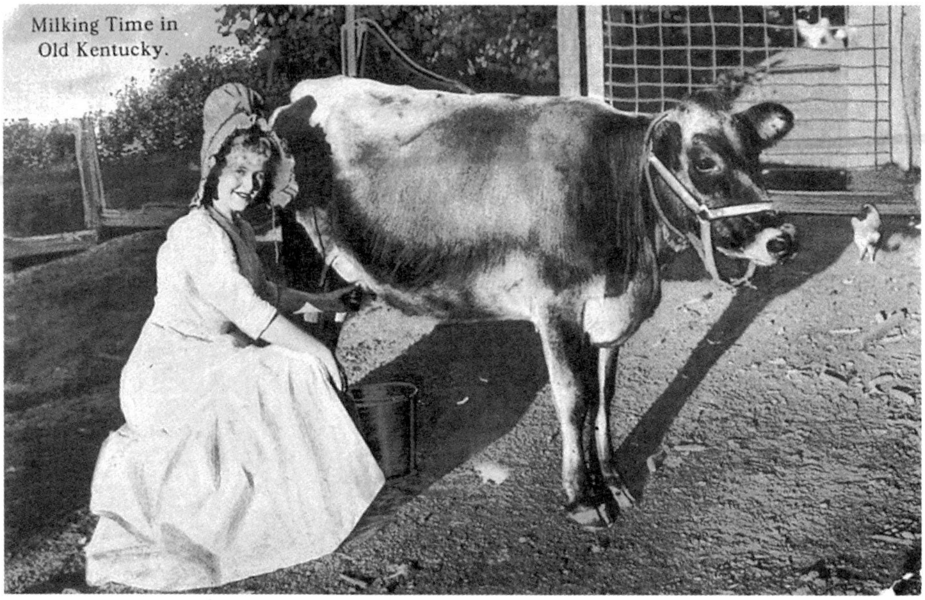

Farm Life is Great
in Old Kentucky,

Corn by Gosh.
In Old Kentucky.

Fire Departments

They have made living safer in cities large and small.

Fire Department in action, Louisville, Ky.

John Fitch

A monument in Bardstown proclaims Fitch, not Robert Fulton, as the inventor of the steamboat.

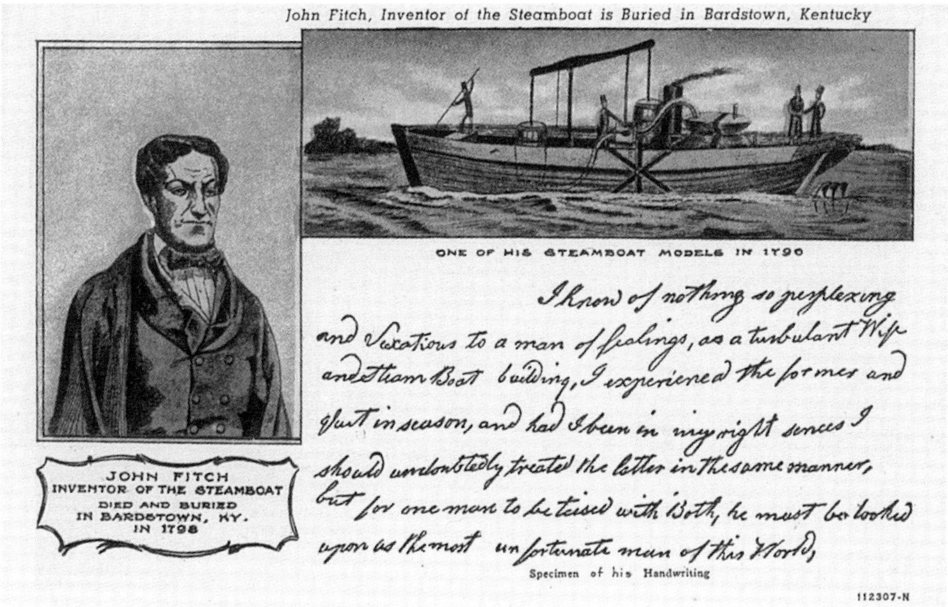

Flemingsburg

The seat of Fleming County, founded in 1797, was once home to James Andrews, a Union spy whose raiders stole a Confederate locomotive in April 1862—inspiration for a famous Buster Keaton movie.

Stephen Collins Foster

According to this portrait card, he wrote "the song that thrills the soul of every Kentuckian."

Frankfort

Originally called Frank's Ford, the city, located on the Kentucky River, is capital of the Commonwealth.

Liberty Hall, Frankfort, Ky. OB-H1395

Third Street, Sen. Paynters Residence, Frankfort, Ky.

Franklin

The Simpson County seat was once renowned for its Mule Day Festival and is now known as a manufacturing center for adhesive tape.

The Frontier Nursing Service

Founded by Mary Breckinridge in 1925 at Hyden, in Leslie County, the FNS has depended upon intrepid nurses, who once rode horseback and now drive the narrow mountain roads—and sometimes get stuck.

Fulton

By the 1920s, this Fulton County town had become a major railroad hub in the Jackson Purchase and soon came to be known as the Banana Crossroads of the United States.

Greetings from Kentucky

A Post Card Tour, 1900-1950

Plate I

Kentucky Trotting Horse and Breeders Association Track,
Lexington, Ky.

KE-10
Guest House of Historic Shaker Village, Kentucky
Shaker Village Guest House
7A-H3274

Plate II

A folding card.

KENTUCKY RIVER, FROM HIGH BRIDGE, AT NIGHT.

FOURTH STREET SOUTH, BY NIGHT, LOUISVILLE, KY.

Plate IV

CUMBERLAND FALLS, KENTUCKY

Bethel Female College, Hopkinsville, Ky.

Abbey of Gethsemane, Nelson County, near Bardstown, Ky.
577-29-N

Harvest Field at Sunset
In Old Kentucky.

No. 9229 Main St., Richmond, Ky.

Logging Train in Kentucky Mountains

Hick's DRIVE-IN RESTAURANT
One mile south of Shively, Ky. on U. S. 31W
Hick's
DRIVE IN
RESTAURANT
Swift's Ice Cream
Hick's
RESTAURANT

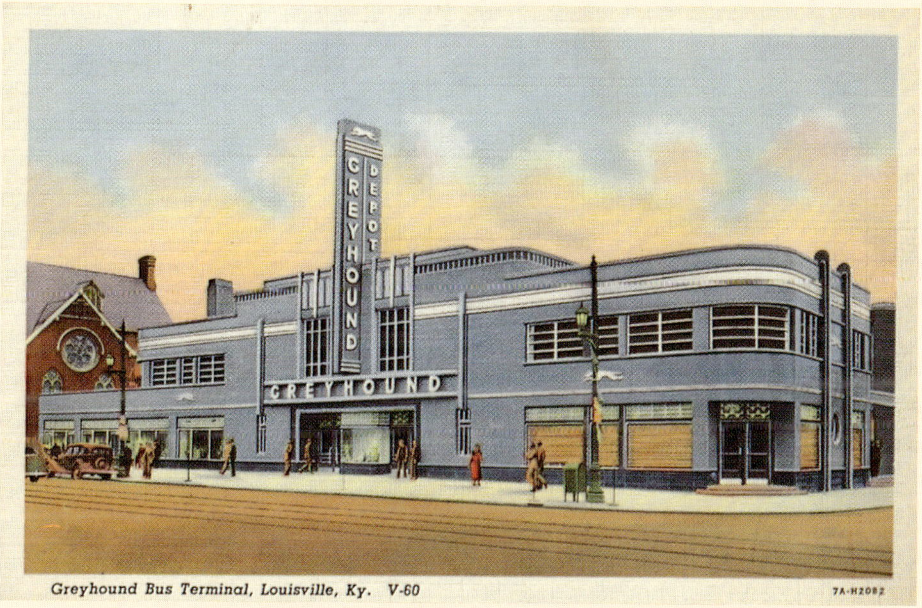
GREYHOUND
DEPOT
GREYHOUND
Greyhound Bus Terminal, Louisville, Ky. V-60
7A-H2082

THE HEART OF BENHAM, KENTUCKY.

U. S. Gold Depository, Fort Knox, Kentucky

Spindletop Stock Farm, Lexington, Ky.

Audubon Memorial Museum, Audubon State Park, Henderson, Kentucky

Plate VIII

G is for . . .

Georgetown
The seat of Scott County was settled by Baptist minister Elijah Craig, who also manufactured rope from hemp and may have invented the process of making bourbon whiskey. The town was named in honor of George Washington and is the home of Georgetown College.

Gethsemani
This Trappist monastery, founded in 1848 ten miles south of Bardstown, was the home of poet and religious writer Thomas Merton from 1941 until his death in 1968.

Ghent

Located across the Ohio River from Vevay, Indiana, this Carroll County town was named, at the suggestion of Henry Clay, for the Belgian city where the treaty ending the War of 1812 was signed.

Glasgow

The Barren County seat was named for the Scottish city from which several of its founding families had come.

BARREN COUNTY COURT HOUSE, GLASGOW, KY. 80353

Court House, Greensburg, Ky. Built 1799.

Greensburg

The seat of Green County, on the Green River, is home of the oldest courthouse west of the Allegheny Mountains.

Greenup

Situated at the confluence of the Ohio and Little Sandy rivers, the town was named for Christopher Greenup, Kentucky's fourth governor (1804-08).

Guthrie

This Todd County town on the Tennessee border was the birthplace of writer Robert Penn Warren.

H is for . . .

Harlan

The Harlan County seat, situated where the Clover and Martins forks of the Cumberland River meet, was originally named Mt. Pleasant.

Harrodsburg

The first permanent settlement in Kentucky, this Mercer County seat was founded in 1774 by James Harrod and named Harrod's Town in his honor.

MAIN STREET, HARRODSBURG, KY.

Hawesville

The seat of Hancock County, on the Ohio River, is now an industrial center.

Hazard

A center of the coal industry, the seat of Perry County is on the North Fork of the Kentucky River.

Hemp

The notorious *Cannabis sativa*, an Asian plant, was once grown widely in Kentucky for its fiber, used in making rope and sailcloth. It is now grown illegally for recreational purposes.

Henderson

During the 1940s this Ohio River manufacturing and trade center, seat of Henderson County, was home to notorious night clubs and gambling casinos.

Hickman

The seat of Fulton County was once an important Mississippi River trading center.

7243 A Portion of West Hickman, Hickman, Ky., Showing Several Factories.

Hindman

The scene of several bloody feuds rooted in the Civil War, this Knott County seat is located at the fork of Troublesome Creek.

Historic sites and monuments

Whether real or imagined, they contribute to Kentucky's romantic and heroic past.

Fort Harrod, Pioneer Memorial State Park, Harrodsburg, Kentucky, showing interior of Fort and old Spring.

Historic sites and monuments

DEDICATING OLD FORT AT HARRODSBURG, KY.

The Old Munford Inn, Munfordville, Ky. Where Pres. Jackson stayed over Night on Way to Washington. Erected Over a Century Ago.

NEAR JUNCTION CITY, HOME OF KENTUCKY'S FIRST GOVERNOR. THE FIRST STONE HOUSE BUILT IN THE STATE.

"Uncle Tom's Cabin
and the House where the Story was Written",
near Lancaster, Ky.

Home of "Mrs. Wiggs of the Cabbage Patch," Louisville, Ky.

Historic sites and monuments

Confederate Monument, Park Place—Louisville

The Old Mill, Bardstown, Ky.

No. 4503 Publ. Atlas Society New York. Made in Germany

Hodgenville

The seat of Larue County, Hodgenville had its courthouse burned in February 1865 by Confederate guerrillas. Nearby is the birthplace of Abraham Lincoln.

Hopkinsville

The Christian County seat was a center of the friction between farmers and buyers during the tobacco wars of the early 1900s.

Horse Cave

The Hart County town is a large burley tobacco market, a manufacturing center, and home to the professional Horse Cave Theatre.

Horses

In Kentucky, horses and everything that goes with them, from farms to racetracks, are major attractions.

KEENELAND ASSOCIATION RUNNING TRACK, LEXINGTON, KY.
6A-H1867

LEAVING THE KEENELAND PADDOCK

Calumet Farm, Lexington, Ky.
8A-H587

Man O'War Statue, Faraway Farm
Lexington, Kentucky
PHOTO BY KNOX OSBORNE
9B-H1266

1909
CLUB HOUSE AND GRAND STAND, LATONIA, KENTUCKY.

Mrs. W. Fine
617 W. Chestnut
Louisville
Ky.
Dear Elsie
4602
LOUISVILLE JOCKEY CLUB, LOUISVILLE, KY.
ILLUSTRATED POST CARD CO., N. Y.
Hope you are having a good time while the races are in town. Stephany

GALLAHADION,
WINNER OF 1940 KENTUCKY DERBY—K68
© CAUFIELD & SHOOK

Race Track from Grand Stand, Latonia, Ky.

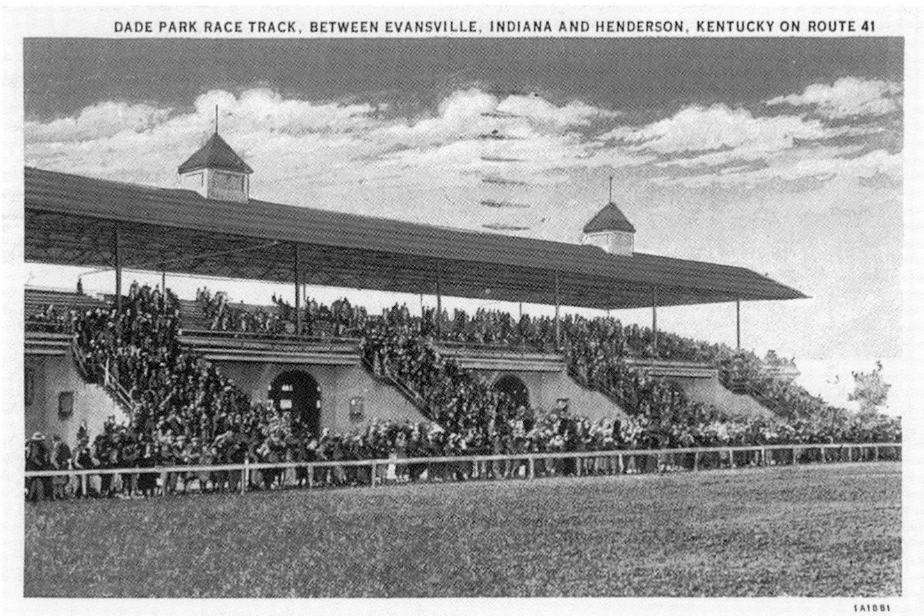
DADE PARK RACE TRACK, BETWEEN EVANSVILLE, INDIANA AND HENDERSON, KENTUCKY ON ROUTE 41
1A1881

Hotels, Motels, and Tourist Cabins

Kentucky's public sleeping accommodations are scattered from Pikeville to Somerset to Hopkinsville to Horse Cave.

HOTEL CHESTERFIELD, BROADWAY AT FIFTH, OPPOSITE BUS STATION, LOUISVILLE, KY.

HOTEL HENRY WATTERSON,
Walnut and Fourth Streets,
LOUISVILLE, KY.
LOUISVILLE, KY.

PHOENIX HOTEL
PHOENIX HOTEL — LEXINGTON, KY.
4A251

"SLEEP IN SAFETY" HOTEL JAMES HATCHER, PIKEVILLE, KY. ONLY FIREPROOF HOTEL ON THE BIG SANDY
ENTRANCE
I CAME HERE FOR A CHANGE AND REST PORTERS GET THE CHANGE AND THE HOTEL GETS THE REST
B-611

Hotels, Motels, and Tourist Cabins

Views of Lobby, Sun Room and Guest Room, Wilbur Hotel, Corbin, Kentucky

STEARNS HOTEL, STEARNS, KENTUCKY.

GENTRY HOTEL, WILLIAMSBURG, KY.
45630

HENRY CLAY HOTEL, LOUISVILLE, KY.
24
© CAUFIELD & SHOOK, LOUISVILLE

9640 Cumberland Falls, Ky. Hotel, H.C.Brunson, Propr.

MAMMOTH CAVE HOTEL, MAMMOTH CAVE, KY.
1A574

Great Onyx Cave Hotel
Copyrighted 1920 by
Bowling Green Ky 1925

BOONE TAVERN
Boone Tavern
Berea, Ky.

A 17045 Capital Hotel, Frankfort, Ky.

NEWTONIAN HOTEL, SOMERSET, KY.

E. C. KROPP, MILWAUKEE

Kinniconick Hotel, Kinniconick, Ky.

1B866-N

The Middlesborough, Middlesborough, Ky.

A ROBERT NOE HOTEL
HOTEL JOPLIN
MARCUMS STORE
CAFE
HOTEL JOPLIN — ELIZABETHTOWN, KY.
2B-H1289

COUNTRY HAM
MOTEL
AAA
LARGEST COUNTRY HAM DISPLAY IN U. S. A.
IN BOWLING GREEN, KENTUCKY ON 31W ALTERNATE
COUNTRY HAM
MOTEL
Tourist
COTTAGES

PART OF THE CABINS IN RENFRO VALLEY SETTLEMENT - RENFRO VALLEY, KY.
CLINE PHOTO
1-Y-358

PEACOCK COTTAGES
PEACOCK
COTTAGES
RESTAURANT
ON U.S. HIGHWAY 42 • GOSHEN, KENTUCKY

Eplee's Tourist Court, Berea, Kentucky — on Highway U. S. 25
B5512

THE SGT. YORK MOTEL - BURNSIDE, KY. - U.S. 27

Where Colonel Sanders began his rise to fame.

Humor

It has a popular appeal with card senders, whether a crudely drawn homemade card or a commercial poke at racetrack betting.

Greetings from LOUISVILLE, KY.
TODAY'S "LONG SHOT" AT
CHURCHILL DOWNS
B

I is for . . .

Industries

Kentucky's modern industries grew from such modest beginnings as gristmills, logging, quarrying, and early iron foundries.

An Old Kentucky Water Mill, near Mount Vernon, Ky.

This is where Zaring's Patent Flour is made, Richmond, Ky.

Logs on Kentucky River, Kentucky.

White Stone Quarry, Bowling Green, Ky.

Industries

Indian Refinery, Georgetown, Ky.

KENTUCKY UTILITIES ELECTRICAL PLANT ON CUMBERLAND RIVER IN KENTUCKY.

Asphalt Mines, near Bowling Green, Ky.

Institutions

They serve the mental, protective, and health needs of Kentuckians across the Commonwealth.

Sanitarium,
Henderson, Ky.

LOUISVILLE. Masonic Widow's and Orphans' Home.

St. Joseph's Infirmary, Louisville, Ky.

Irvine

The seat of Estill County, located on the Kentucky River, was the scene of several skirmishes during the Civil War.

J is for . . .

Richard M. Johnson

Born on Beargrass Creek near Louisville, Johnson was reputed to be the slayer of Chief Tecumseh at the Battle of the Thames in 1813 and later served as vice-president of the United States (1837-41).

Junction City

The small town in Boyle County near Danville was first called Goresburg.

K is for . . .

Kentucky

The Land Beyond the Mountains, the New Eden, the Dark and Bloody Ground, the Land of Tomorrow, the Mother of the West, the Fifteenth Star of the Union—Kentucky has been all these and more to citizens and visitors through two centuries.

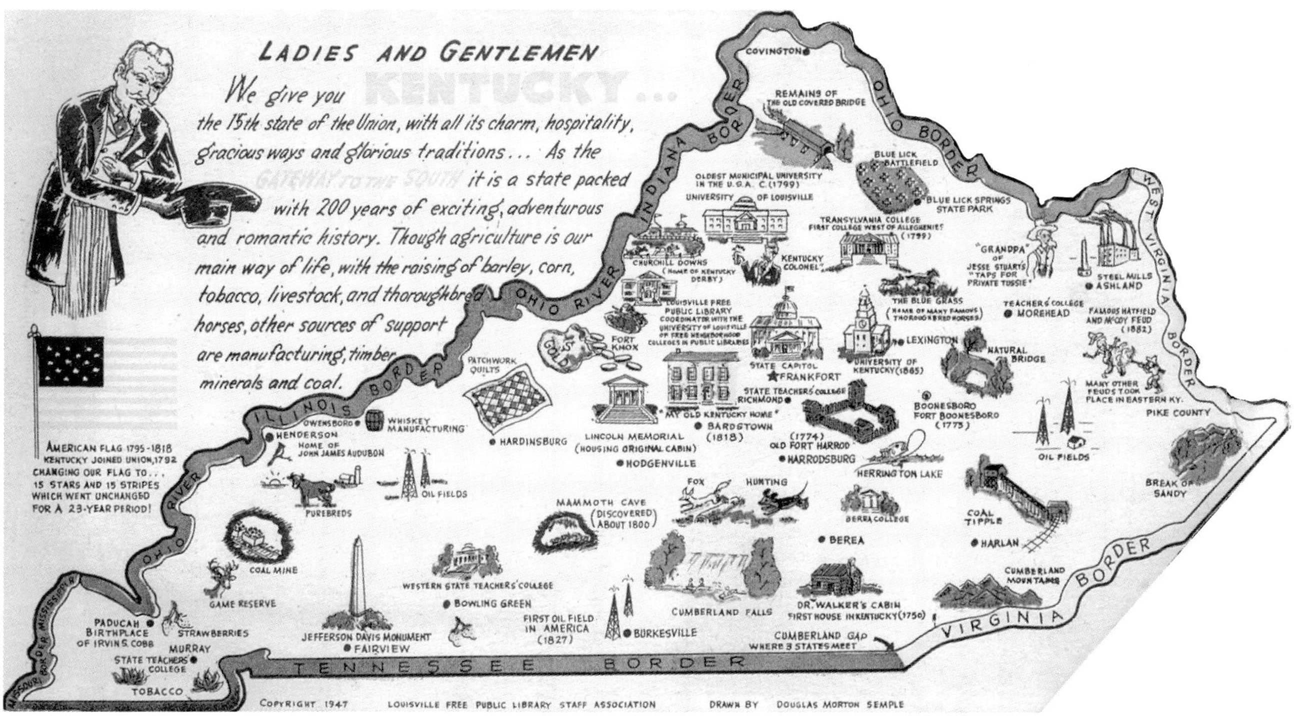

Kentucky Historical Society

Founded in 1836 to collect and preserve precious fragments of Kentucky's past, the Society was located from 1909 to 1920 in the new Capitol, as this card shows. It now occupies the Old State Capitol in Frankfort.

KENTUCKY HISTORICAL SOCIETY ROOM IN THE NEW STATE CAPITOL, FRANKFORT, KY.

Kentucky River

A major transportation system since prehistoric times, the river flows almost 255 miles from Beattyville northwesterly to join the Ohio River at Carrollton.

Kentucky State Fair

These cards show the annual fair during the years when it was located in Louisville's West End, 1908 to 1956

Kentucky stereotypes

Many a post card oversimplified, exaggerated, or distorted state images and assets.

Two Typical Kentuckians
Personality and Mint Julep
Relics almost extinct—
K28

My Old Kentucky Home.

L is for . . .

La Grange

The seat of Oldham County was named for the country estate of the Marquis de Lafayette, French hero of the American Revolution, who toured Kentucky in 1825.

Lawrenceburg

The Anderson County seat was named in 1820 for a local tavern owner.

Lebanon

An early railroad center, Lebanon, the seat of Marion County, had eight southbound and seven northbound trains passing through daily in 1859.

MAIN STREET, LOOKING WEST, BY NIGHT, LEBANON, KY.

Lexington

Kentucky's second largest city, known in the 1820s as "the Athens of the West," is world renowned as a center for the breeding and sale of Thoroughbred and Standardbred horses.

Bird's Eye View showing West Main Street Viaduct, Lexington, Ky.

A 17073 Main Street, Lexington, Ky.

Scene on Main Street, looking West, showing
New Fayette Bank Building in distance,
Lexington, Ky.
RAINCOAT SALE

Historical Bryan Station Spring
near Lexington, Ky.

Fayette County Court House Lexington, Ky.

Abraham Lincoln

Born near Hodgenville in 1908 but living most of his life in Indiana and Illinois, Lincoln retained close connections with his native state. In 1842 he married Mary Todd of Lexington.

Replica of Abraham Lincoln's Boyhood Home,
Knob Creek, Ky.
9A355

In Old Kentucky, where the grass grows green,
An old log cabin may yet be seen;
It sheltered a Life that Fate had decreed
Should come at the call of the Country's need.
By the light of the fire, in the twilight hour;
The lad wove his dreams, asking God for power,
His soul longed for wisdom and drank in rich lore
Til his mind was filled with a wondrous store.
God called for a Man when the bravest might shrink;
The Good Ship of State seemed ready to sink.
God guided the Pilot, who stood at the Wheel
With eyes on the Future, and heart true as steel.
The Union we love is a monument grand
To Abraham Lincoln – long, long may it stand!
"I'll study and be ready and maybe the chance will come."

LINCOLN STATUE, COURT SQUARE, HODGENVILLE, KY.

LINCOLN CABIN, INSIDE MEMORIAL HALL, ON LINCOLN FARM, NEAR HODGENVILLE, KY.

London

The seat of Laurel County was settled at midpoint on the Wilderness Road and was the site of a Confederate victory in August 1862.

Louisa

Where the Tug and Levisa forks meet to form the Big Sandy River sits Louisa, seat of Lawrence County.

Louisville

Kentucky's largest city, a manufacturing, financial, arts, and medical center, was founded by George Rogers Clark at the Falls of the Ohio in 1778 and named to honor the ill-fated Louis XVI of France because of his support for the colonies during the American Revolution.

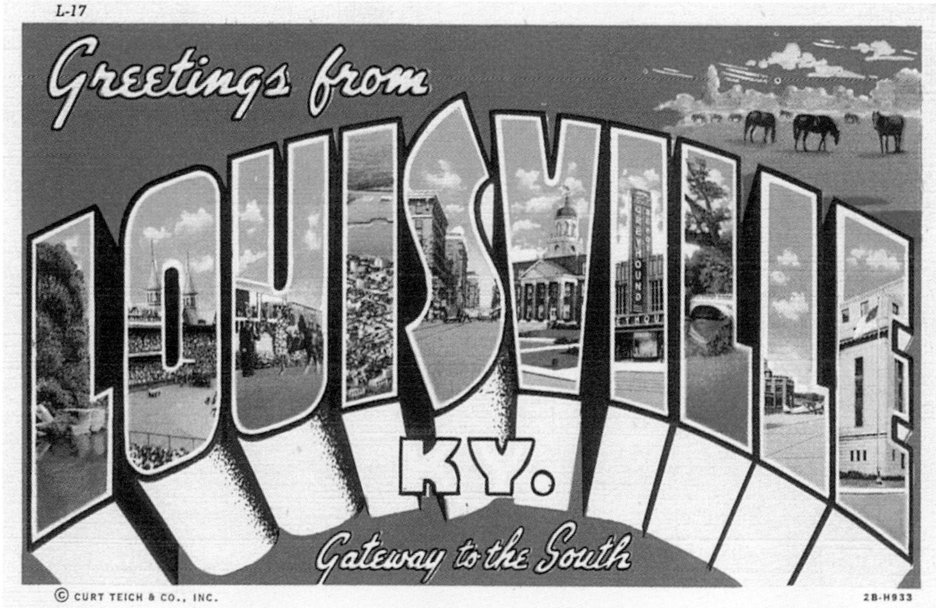

Louisville

Courier Journal Building, Louisville, Ky.

Custom House and Post Office,
View from Third Avenue and Chestnut Street,
Louisville, Ky.
STANDARD CLEANING CO.

City Hall, Louisville, Kentucky.

View on 4th Ave bet Green & Walnut Sts.–Louisville

FOURTH AVE. SHOWING FEDERAL BLDG.,
LOUISVILLE, KY.
B.F.
KEITH'S
VAUDEVILLE

View of 4th Ave, Louisville. Ky.
ATLANTIC

L-10—Broadway Looking East, Louisville, Ky.
GREYHOUND
DEPOT
2B-H930

Copyright 1906 by the Rotograph Co.
G 17107 Court House, Louisville, Ky.

M is for . . .

Madisonville
Kentucky governor Ruby Laffoon (1931-35) hailed from Madisonville, the seat of Hopkins County.

Mammoth Cave National Park
The state's only national park is the site of one of the world's most famous natural wonders. The park opened in 1941, but the cave has attracted millions of sightseers since the early nineteenth century.

Mayfield

The Graves County seat was settled in 1819 and was a Confederate center during the Civil War. Recently it was the setting for native Bobbie Ann Mason's *In Country*, a novel (and movie) about a young girl's search for her father killed in the Vietnam War.

Maysville

An entrance for pioneers into the interior of Kentucky, Maysville, seat of Mason County, lies at the confluence of Limestone Creek and the Ohio River.

Ephraim McDowell

McDowell was a Virginia-born surgeon who made medical history by performing the first successful ovariotomy in Danville on Christmas Day 1809.

Middlesboro

Founded as a "planned city" in 1890 at the base of Cumberland Gap by Scottish entrepreneur Alexander Alan Arthur, Middlesboro was designed to exploit the area's natural resources.

Military

The military tradition has long been honored in Kentucky, which has sent soldiers to fight in all the nation's wars.

Wash Day at Camp Zachary Taylor, Louisville, Ky.

Military

Camp Zachary Taylor, Louisville, during World War I

Interior of Service Club No. 2, Camp Campbell, Ky.-Tenn.
2B-H1276

LOUISVILLE'S SERVICE CLUB
SERVICE CLUB
824 SOUTH FOURTH STREET — LOUISVILLE 3, KY.
2B-H928

The Stop-Over Station No. 1 Lexington, Kentucky
← Section of the main Lounge. Books of all kinds, the latest magazines and periodicals are found. Radios and writing materials are furnished and a homey atmosphere prevails.
Corner of the Play Room. Billiards, ping pong, checkers, jig saw puzzles and other games are furnished. →
← Kitchen and serving counter. Wholesome food is prepared and served to all men and women in service without charge. Tables are provided for their comfort.
Corner of sleeping quarters. Nice clean sleeping facilities are provided without cost for all who desire it. Women's sleeping quarters next door. →
For Those In The Armed Forces

Officers Country Club, Fort Knox, Ky.
OB-H1938

COPYRIGHT 1907 BY DETROIT PUBLISHING CO.
11475. THE BARRACKS, FORT THOMAS, KY.

GENERAL VIEW LOOKING NORTH FROM OBSERVATION TOWER.
Photo Hesse. Official Photog. U. S. Gov
U. S. NATIONAL ARMY CANTONMENT, CAMP ZACHARY TAYLOR, LOUISVILLE, KY.

Moonshine

This traditional beverage, venerated and consumed for two hundred years, has undone many a Kentuckian and created a vast body of folklore.

John Hunt Morgan

The "Thunderbolt of the Confederacy," a Lexington native, led cavalry raids from Tennessee into Kentucky, Indiana, and Ohio in 1862 and 1863.

Morganfield

The seat of Union County was built around Morgan Springs, which provided settlers with plentiful water.

Mountains

The far eastern region of Kentucky is part of the Appalachian system, with Big Black Mountain in Harlan County the highest point in the state. The region's long isolation fostered a distinctive culture.

Mountains

Mt. Sterling

The seat of Montgomery County was originally called Little Mountain Town after a large Indian mound nearby.

Mt. Vernon

This important stop for pioneers on the Wilderness Road into Kentucky is now the seat of Rockcastle County.

Murray

The seat of Calloway County has been called Williston, Pooltown, Pleasant Hill, and, since 1844, Murray. Murray Normal School, now Murray State University, was established in 1922.

Music

From folk ballads to Bluegrass to the popular country style performed at Renfro Valley in Rockcastle County, music has been a favorite pastime of Kentuckians for generations.

Jean Thomas, nicknamed "The Traipsin' Woman," a mountain music promoter and folklore collector from Ashland.

BIRTH PLACE OF BRADLEY KINCAID, THE FAMOUS OLD MOUNTAIN BALLAD SINGER
NEAR THE VILLAGE OF POINT LEAVELL, GARRARD COUNTY, "IN OLD KENTUCKY"

N is for . . .

Natural Bridge

This natural arch in Powell County, one of many in Kentucky, is just one of the state's outdoor wonders.

Newport

Located on the Ohio River across from Cincinnati, Newport is, with Alexandria, one of the two seats of Campbell County. It was a gambling center from the 1930s through the 1950s.

CITY OFFICES AND COURT HOUSE, NEWPORT, KY.

Nicholasville

Within several days in 1862, the seat of Jessamine County provided almost a thousand men for John Hunt Morgan's Confederate cavalry.

Main Street, Nicholasville, Ky.

Night Riders

Between 1905 and 1909, farmers in Western Kentucky organized a vigilante movement to withhold tobacco from the market and force up prices.

IN THE NIGHT RIDER DISTRICT OF KENTUCKY TROOPERS GOING ON DUTY.

O is for . . .

Theodore O'Hara

The Danville native was author of the famous poem "The Bivouac of the Dead," written to honor Kentuckians who fell in the Mexican War.

The resting place of Theodore O'Hara
Author of The Bivouac of the Dead.
Frankfort, Ky.

Ohio River

Formed by the confluence of the Allegheny and Monongahela rivers at Pittsburgh, the Ohio borders Kentucky for 665 miles, from Catlettsburg to Cairo, Illinois. The Falls at Louisville constituted the only barrier to navigation, overcome by the opening of the Louisville and Portland Canal in 1830.

Wharf Boat, Augusta, Ky.

Ohio River Falls, Louisville, Ky.

Indiana Chute, Ohio River, Louisville, Ky.

COPYRIGHT, 1905, BY DETROIT PUBLISHING CO.
TRANSIT
LOUISVILLE KY.
10432.
The water is a muddy brown not green H.

Ohio River

Dam from middle of the Ohio River, Louisville, Ky.

Moonlight on the Ohio River, Louisville, Ky.
7A-H224

U. S. COAST GUARD STATION. THE ONLY INLAND LIFE-SAVING STATION IN AMERICA. LOUISVILLE, KY. 13
© CAUFIELD & SHOOK, LOUISVILLE

QUEEN CITY BEACH, BELLEVUE, KY. OPPOSITE CINCINNATI, O.

A SCENE ON THE OHIO RIVER, HAWESVILLE, KY.

Owensboro

The seat of Daviess County, on the Ohio River and originally called Yellow Banks, now bills itself as "the Barbecue Capital of the World."

P is for . . .

Paducah

Purportedly named for the legendary Cherokee chief Paduke, the seat of McCracken County lies at the junction of the Tennessee and Ohio rivers.

Paris

The seat of Bourbon County, originally named Hopewell, is a major tobacco market.

Parksville

The Boyle County town is at the head of the Chaplin River.

People

Myriad Kentuckians celebrated their families, friends, and themselves with Real Photo post cards.

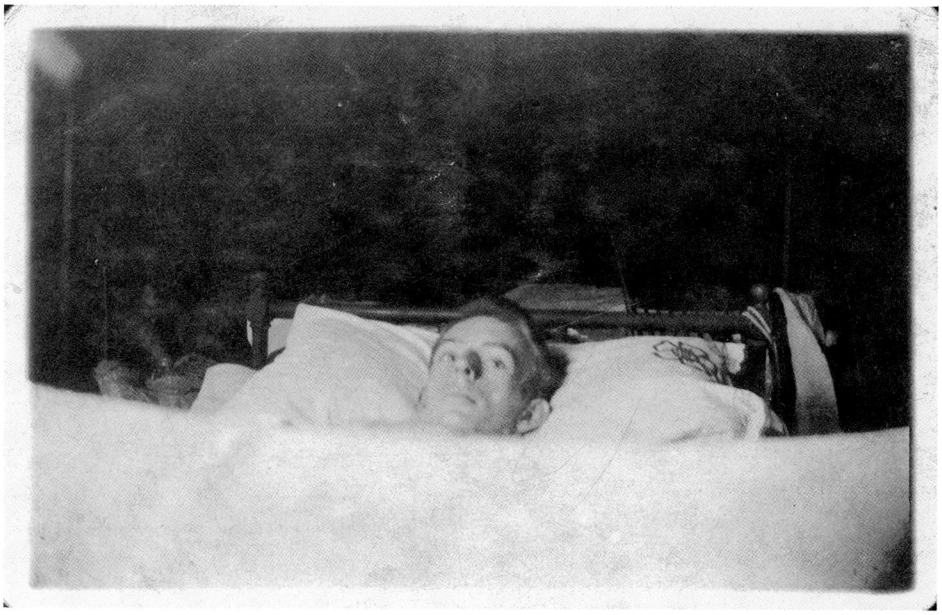

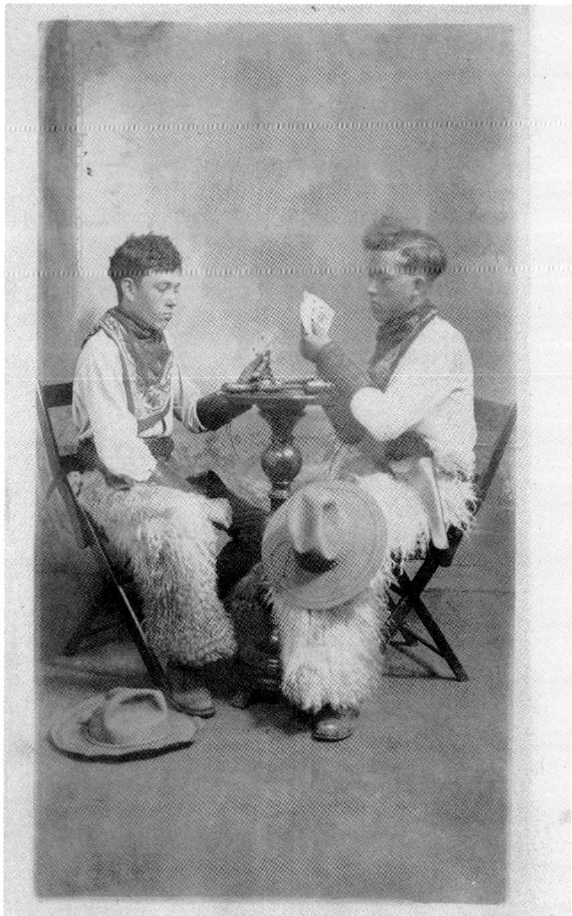

Pewee Valley

This Oldham County community, located on a ridge, not in a valley, was supposedly named for a flock of pewees, or phoebes, that serenaded the meeting called to choose a town name.

Pikeville

The Pike County seat gained almost four hundred acres of new land in 1987 when the Levisa Fork of the Big Sandy River was diverted from its normal route through town.

Pineville

The seat of Bell County, on the Cumberland River, was known as Cumberland Ford when it was settled in 1781. The Mountain Laurel Festival is now an annual event.

Poetry

Kentuckians write it in great abundance, some of it very good and some of it motivated by love of the homeland.

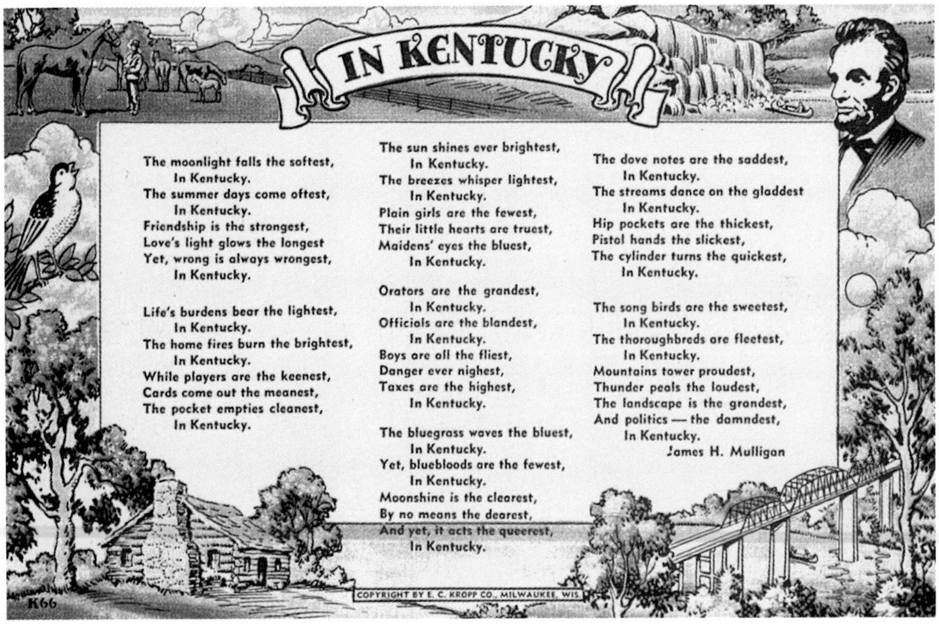

IN KENTUCKY

The moonlight falls the softest,
In Kentucky.
The summer days come oftest,
In Kentucky.
Friendship is the strongest,
Love's light glows the longest
Yet, wrong is always wrongest,
In Kentucky.

Life's burdens bear the lightest,
In Kentucky.
The home fires burn the brightest,
In Kentucky.
While players are the keenest,
Cards come out the meanest,
The pocket empties cleanest,
In Kentucky.

The sun shines ever brightest,
In Kentucky.
The breezes whisper lightest,
In Kentucky.
Plain girls are the fewest,
Their little hearts are truest,
Maidens' eyes the bluest,
In Kentucky.

Orators are the grandest,
In Kentucky.
Officials are the blandest,
In Kentucky.
Boys are all the fliest,
Danger ever nighest,
Taxes are the highest,
In Kentucky.

The bluegrass waves the bluest,
In Kentucky.
Yet, bluebloods are the fewest,
In Kentucky.
Moonshine is the clearest,
By no means the dearest,
And yet, it acts the queerest,
In Kentucky.

The dove notes are the saddest,
In Kentucky.
The streams dance on the gladdest
In Kentucky.
Hip pockets are the thickest,
Pistol hands the slickest,
The cylinder turns the quickest,
In Kentucky.

The song birds are the sweetest,
In Kentucky.
The thoroughbreds are fleetest,
In Kentucky.
Mountains tower proudest,
Thunder peals the loudest,
The landscape is the grandest,
And politics — the damndest,
In Kentucky.

James H. Mulligan

COPYRIGHT BY E. C. KROPP CO., MILWAUKEE, WIS.

K66

"In Falmouth"

Kentucky's fairs are fairest
In Falmouth;
The premiums are the squarest
In Falmouth;
The crowds they gather thickest,
The "speelers" are the slickest,
Your money leaves you quickest
In Falmouth.

Fair weather is the fairest
In Falmouth;
Slow times are the rarest
In Falmouth;
The speakers are the brightest,
Hard feelings are the slightest,
Friendship ties are tightest
In Falmouth.

The horses are the fleetest
In Falmouth;
The orange cider sweetest
In Falmouth;
The skies are the bluest,
The judges' decisions truest,
Disappointed people fewest
In Falmouth.

Kentucky's fairs are fairest
In Falmouth;
Slow times are rarest
In Falmouth;
The bad are never badest,
The sad are never sadest,
But the glad are always gladest
In Falmouth.

APPLEGATE & WILSON, PUB.

"Old Kaintuck"

[It is remarkable what fraternal relation exists among Kentuckians, especially where they meet in foreign States and away from home; and their loyalty to each other has been occasion for many kindly comments on the part of the outside world, who marvel at the brotherhood that exists among Kentuckians, wherever found.---*Thomas H. Arnold, of Chicago.*]

YOU'RE just from old Kaintucky?
Well, I'll be gol durned---say,
I'd rather live in that State
The balance of my days
Than be the Czar of Russia
With his riches and his truck---
Say, I wouldn't take his kingdom
For one corner of old Kaintuck.

I'D rather be a hopper,
Jus' lazin' in the corn
On an old Kaintucky hillside
Than any king that's born.
I'd rather watch the bluegrass
Nod its dainty head and bow,
Than see the slickest pictur,
In old Italy, I swow.

IT seems to me old Natur'
When she cut Kaintucky out,
Came pretty near a-knowin'
The thing she was about.
So she made another Eden
With the sweetest flowers that grew,
And christened it Kaintucky
With a jug of mountain dew.

THERE ain't no other corner
Of this old hemisphere of ours,
Where old Mother Earth is kivered
With such dainty, perfumed flowers;
Whar the teeter-birds and thrushes
Can ejaculate such notes
As they can in old Kentucky,
From their little feathered throats.

AND the women, jumpin' jay birds, in the good old Bluegrass State:
The Lord just made 'em perfect, and lost the fashion plate;
I wouldn't be without 'em---and I'll stay here by-the-bye---
You can plant me in Kaintucky, when it comes my time to die.

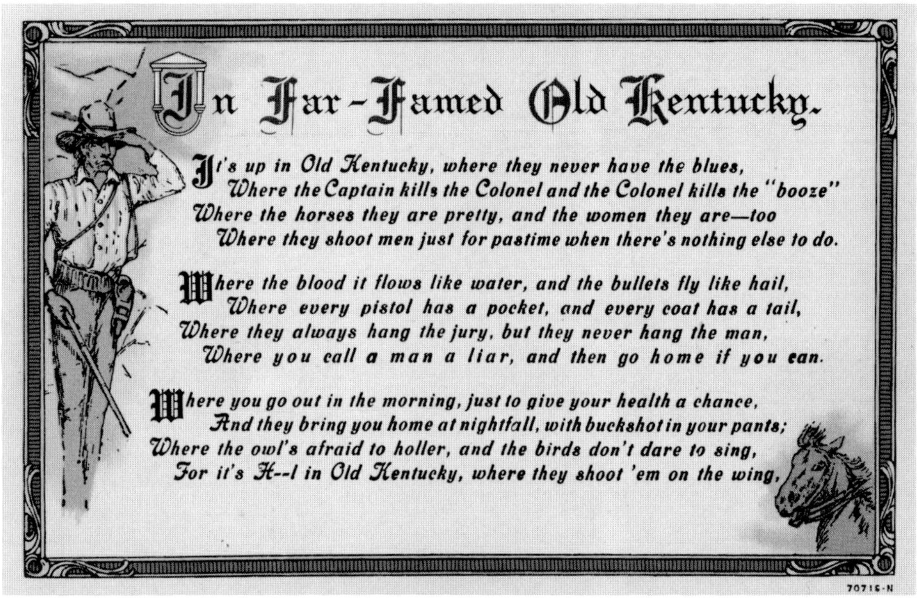

In Far-Famed Old Kentucky.

It's up in Old Kentucky, where they never have the blues,
Where the Captain kills the Colonel and the Colonel kills the "booze"
Where the horses they are pretty, and the women they are—too
Where they shoot men just for pastime when there's nothing else to do.

Where the blood it flows like water, and the bullets fly like hail,
Where every pistol has a pocket, and every coat has a tail,
Where they always hang the jury, but they never hang the man,
Where you call a man a liar, and then go home if you can.

Where you go out in the morning, just to give your health a chance,
And they bring you home at nightfall, with buckshot in your pants;
Where the owl's afraid to holler, and the birds don't dare to sing,
For it's H--l in Old Kentucky, where they shoot 'em on the wing.

70716-N

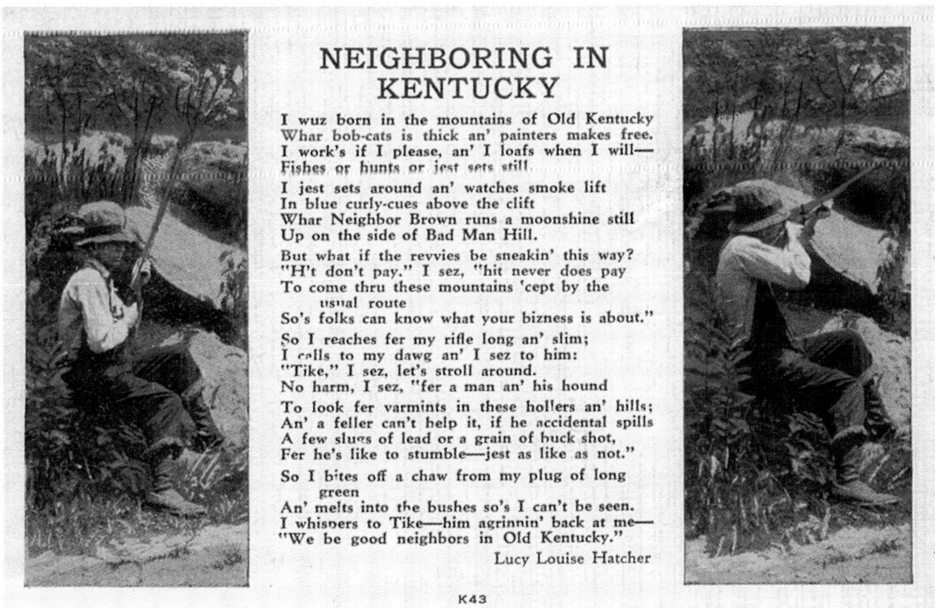

NEIGHBORING IN KENTUCKY

I wuz born in the mountains of Old Kentucky
Whar bob-cats is thick an' painters makes free.
I work's if I please, an' I loafs when I will—
Fishes or hunts or jest sets still.

I jest sets around an' watches smoke lift
In blue curly-cues above the clift
Whar Neighbor Brown runs a moonshine still
Up on the side of Bad Man Hill.

But what if the revvies be sneakin' this way?
"H't don't pay," I sez, "hit never does pay
To come thru these mountains 'cept by the
usual route
So's folks can know what your bizness is about."

So I reaches fer my rifle long an' slim;
I calls to my dawg an' I sez to him:
"Tike," I sez, let's stroll around.
No harm, I sez, "fer a man an' his hound

To look fer varmints in these hollers an' hills;
An' a feller can't help it, if he accidental spills
A few slugs of lead or a grain of buck shot,
Fer he's like to stumble—jest as like as not."

So I bites off a chaw from my plug of long
green
An' melts into the bushes so's I can't be seen.
I whispers to Tike—him agrinnin' back at me—
"We be good neighbors in Old Kentucky."

Lucy Louise Hatcher

K43

After a Visit to Old Kentucky

I be'n in ole Kentucky
  Fur a week er two, an' say,
'Twuz ez hard ez breakin' oxen
  Fur to tear myse'f away.
Allus argerin' 'bout fr'en'ship
  An' yer hospitality---
Y' ain't no right to talk about it
  Tell you be'n down there to see.

SEE jest how they give you welcome
  To the best that's in the land.
Feel the sort o' grip they give you
  When they take you by the hand.
Hear 'em say, "We're glad to have you.
  Better stay a week er two;"
An' the way they treat you makes you
  Feel that ev'ry word is true.

FEED you tell you hear the buttons
  Crackin' on yore Sunday vest;
Haul you roun' to see the wonders
  Tell you have to cry for rest.
Drink yer health an' pet an' praise you
  Tell you git to feel ez great
Ez the Sheriff o' the county
  Er the Gov'ner o' the State.

WIFE, she says I must be crazy
  Cause I go on so, an' Nelse
He 'lows, "Goodness gracious! daddy,
  Cain't you talk about nuthin' else?"
Well, pleg-gone it, I'm jes' tickled--
  Bein' tickled ain't no sin:
I be'n down in ole Kentucky,
  An' I wan' o' go ag'in.

70717-N

GOD LIVES IN KENTUCKY

John A. Logan

God is good to Indiana
  As a father to his child,
But he made our Old Kentucky
  And he just looked at her and smiled.
Then he made the broad Ohio
  Circle 'round this land so fair.
As a mother hugs her baby
  To her heart with tender care.
Yes, God went to Indiana
  And he blessed each hill and glade;
But he came down to Kentucky
  And just sat down here and stayed.
Here he made Davis and Lincoln,
  Destined each to play his part;
And a sacrifice so noble,
  Healed a nation's broken heart.
And George Rogers Clark he sent with
  His Kentucky rifle band,
To release his Indiana
  From the English tyrants hand.
Then he sent old Davy Crockett
  'Way out to the Alamo
And they made the State of Texas
  Out of Northern Mexico.
Here he heard the call of Jackson
  'Way down South of New Orleans,
And he sent Kentucky soldiers
  Uniformed in home-made jeans.
When, because each one sought freedom,
  War between the States was made,
To the South he sent Jeff Davis
  To the North Old Honest Abe.
So the Lord sends from Kentucky
  Just the man he wants to go,
Who will do his bidding,
  Everytime—Is it not so?
We believe our God will tell you,
  Tho forever you may roam,
That the nearest place to Heaven
  Is the "Old Kentucky Home."
It is just as clear as can be
  That God loves and freely gives
To the other States His blessings;
  But Kentucky's where he lives.

Politics

The poet says they're "the damndest in Kentucky," where candidates have promoted themselves with whiskey, gingerbread, and even post cards. This Hardin County man's 1930s platform was stated thusly on the reverse side: "A hearty welcome and courteous treatment to my constituents. Ice water in 'The good old Summer time,' and a good fire for you in the Winter."

Post Offices

Whether in a small town or a large city, the post office has always been an important communications center.

405 The Post Office at West Point, Ky., needs repairs before handling mail.

Prisons

They're a necessary evil from one end of the state to the other.

The "Colored" Dining Hall, State Prison, Frankfort

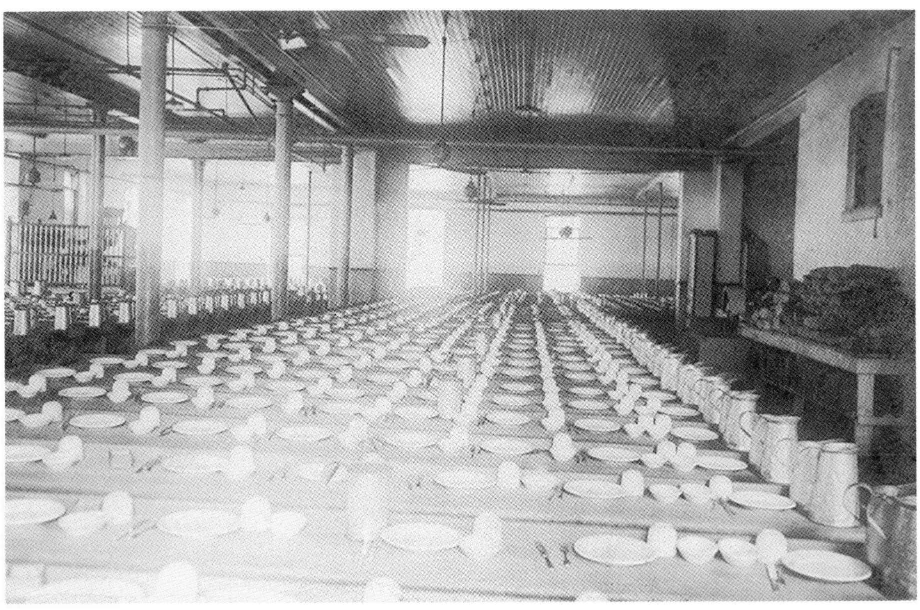

Q is for . . .

Quilts

This Kentucky folk art still warms people of all ages, provides the makers with an artistic outlet, and makes a convenient photographer's backdrop.

The Graveyard Quilt made by Elizabeth Mitchell of Lewis County in 1839. Coffins wait to be moved into the center graveyard as their owners die.

R is for . . .

Restaurants and Other Eateries

They serve Kentucky's famous food, from fried chicken and chess pie to Hot Browns and sizzling steaks, in towns and cities and along roadsides.

Restaurants and Other Eateries

GYPSY GRILL, OFFICIAL GREYHOUND BUS STOP, CARROLLTON, KY. H-487

Baskett's Restaurant, Nicholasville

Coffee Shop, the Old Talbott Tavern, Bardstown, Ky.

U. S. 60, 22 Miles East of Louisville, Kentucky

Ye Olde Stone Inne ~ Simpsonville, Kentucky

Corner in the Dining Room—
Masonic Widows' and Orphans' Home,
Louisville, Ky.

CHIMNEY CORNER
RESTAURANT
1573 Bardstown Road
In the heart of the Highlands
Louisville, Ky.

Roof Garden
The Seelbach, Louisville, Ky.

SMITH CAFE
SMITH CAFE "HOME OF SIZZLING STEAKS"
FULTON, KENTUCKY, ON U. S. HIGHWAYS 45, 51 AND 94

Richmond

The seat of Madison County, settled in 1785, was once the home of Henry Allen Laine, a prominent black poet. It is now home to Eastern Kentucky University.

Roads

Kentucky's roads have progressed from Indian trails and Boone's Wilderness Road to a spacious network of interstate highways. These roads lie somewhere in between.

On road to Glen Lily, near Munfordville, Ky.

One of Kentucky's World Famous Oiled Roads.

A TYPICAL BLUE GRASS ROAD NEAR LEXINGTON, KY.

Road building near Burr in the 1920s

Russellville

The Logan County seat was home to four Kentucky governors: John Breathitt (1832-34), James T. Morehead (1834-36), John J. Crittenden (1848-50), and Charles S. Morehead (1855-59). In 1868 the local bank was robbed by the Jesse James gang.

S is for . . .

Shakers

This celibate religious order, officially known as the Society of Believers, established Kentucky colonies at Pleasant Hill near Harrodsburg and at South Union near Bowling Green.

Old Shaker Mill, near Shakertown, Ky.

A stairway at South Union Shaker village

Shelbyville

The seat of Shelby County was named to honor Kentucky's first governor, Isaac Shelby (1792-96).

Somerset

Founded in 1801 and named by early settlers for a county in New Jersey, the seat of Pulaski County has been a center of tourism since the creation of Lake Cumberland in 1951 and more recently has become an important regional medical center.

Sparta

Located in Gallatin and Owen counties, the town was probably named for a gristmill, Sparta Mill.

Sports and Other Pastimes

From baseball to open-air theaters, Kentuckians find enjoyment in the out-of-doors.

NEW SWIMMING POOL, SHELBY PARK, LOUISVILLE, KY.

WHITE CITY, LOUISVILLE, KY.

13431 Fountain Ferry Park, Louisville, Ky.

Sports and Other Pastimes

Taylorsville's First Fair, 1908, Taylorsville, Ky.

A Kentucky fishing party and their catch

Camp-fire after a Fox Chase in Kentucky.

BASE BALL GRANDSTAND—PROCTOR KNOTT CHAUTAUQUA
LEBANON, KY

MAIN BUILDING AND ENTRANCE, KENTUCKY REPTILE GARDEN, PARK CITY, KY.
KENTUCKY REPTILE GARDEN
MUSEUM

Springfield

The seat of Washington County was the home of writer Elizabeth Madox Roberts.

Springs

These vacation resorts, also known as spas, dotted Kentucky in the nineteenth and early twentieth centuries, offering entertainment and respite from summer heat as well as supposed health cures.

THE NEW GRAHAM SPRINGS HOTEL, HARRODSBURG, KY.

Old Swimmin' Hole
Grayson Springs Ky.

Sebree Springs and Hotel, Sebree, Ky.

Springs

Greetings from Olympian Springs, Olympia, Ky.
The Hotel

Beula Villa Hotel,
Sulphur Well, Ky.

Blue Rock Springs Hotel, Fisherville, Ky.

MASSEY SPRINGS HOTEL
THE MINERAL SPRINGS
MASSEY SPRINGS Ky.
7131

FLOWER GARDEN, CRAB ORCHARD SPRINGS, KY.

© The Standard Printing Co., Inc., Lou., Ky.

OLD SALT WELL.
Blue Lick Springs, Ky.
Where Pioneers made their Salt. - In this enclosure, prehistoric Animal Bones were unearthed, and now on display in Blue Lick Battlefield State Park Museum.

W. I. HAMBY, THE PIONEER AND DISCOVERER OF DAWSON SPRINGS WATER.

Stanford

The seat of Lincoln County was settled by Benjamin Logan in 1775 on St. Asaph Creek.

MAIN STREET, Stanford, Ky.

Steamboats

Only a few relics remain from the hundreds of steamboats that plied Kentucky's waters from 1811 to their heyday in the 1850s and down to the middle of the twentieth century.

Steamboats

4576. Steamer, " City of Louisville, "
Louisville, Ky.
LOUISVI

STEAMBOAT RACE ON THE OHIO RIVER, LOUISVILLE, KY.
V52
CAUFIELD&SHOOK
39096

The Sprague at Shawnee Park,
Largest and Most Handsomely-Appointed Towboat on Inland Waters,
Louisville, Ky.
SPRAGUE

Barton Stone

Stone was one of the founders of the Christian Church, which grew out of a series of camp meetings at Cane Ridge, Bourbon County, in 1801.

Jesse Stuart

Kentucky's beloved author was born and lived his entire life at W-Hollow near Greenup.

T is for . . .

Taylorsville

The seat of Spencer County lies at the confluence of Brashears Creek and the Salt River, which was impounded in 1982 to form Taylorsville Lake.

Theaters

Kentucky's play-houses have seen performances of Greek and Shakespearean classics as well as the most recent Pulitzer Prize dramas.

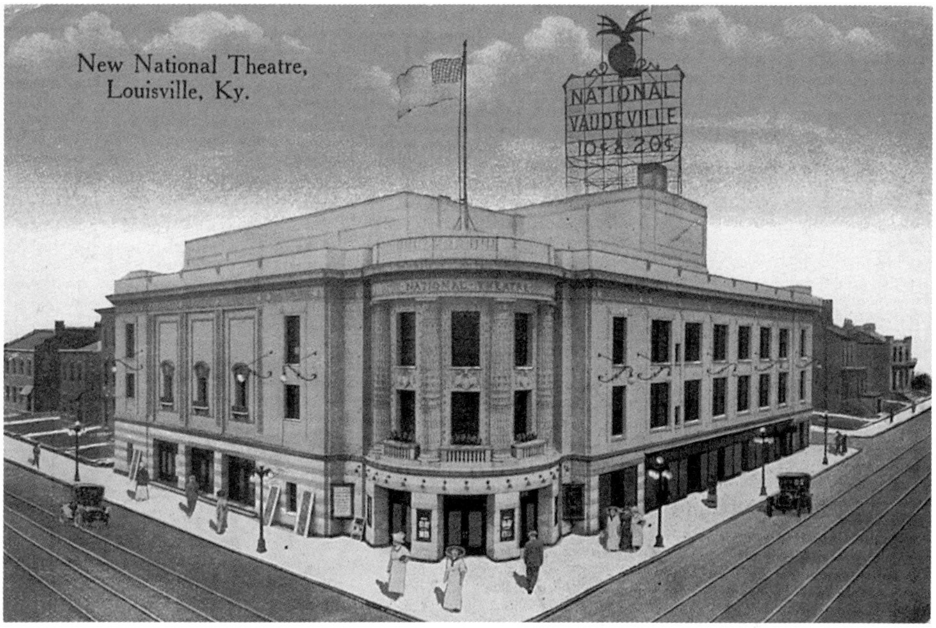

New National Theatre, Louisville, Ky.

Stewart Opera House, Elizabethtown, Kentucky.

Tobacco

The fragrant weed has been a significant part of Kentucky's culture and economy from prehistoric times.

Farmers bringing in thousands upon thousands of pounds of tobacco to be sold in Lexington, Ky., the largest tobacco market in the World.

"THE LARGEST TOBACCO MARKET IN THE WORLD"
INTERIOR OF
O WAREHOUSE, LEXINGTON, KY.

THE TOBACCO CENTER OF THE WORLD, STREET SCENE IN WHOLESALE TOBACCO DISTRICT, LOUISVILLE, KY.

Travel and Transportation

Kentuckians have moved about from here to yonder in many ways—by stagecoach, steamboat, ferry, train, automobile, bus, and airplane.

Stage Coach still in use in the Mountain Section of Kentucky, Burnside and Monticello Stage Line.

Ferry at New Richmond from Kentucky Side.

The Ferry on the Kentucky River, near Winchester, Ky.—7

Decorating the L. & N. Work Train on its Arrival Near Hazard, Ky.

MAMMOTH CAVE R. R. CO.
HERCULES
"HERCULES", FAMOUS ENGINE ON OLD MAMMOTH CAVE R. R. V-408
6A37

10424. FOURTH AVENUE, LOUISVILLE, KY.

Travel and Transportation

VIEW. STEAMER HOMER SMITH, LARGEST EXCURSION BOAT ON OHIO RIVER, MAYSVILLE, KY. 58322

U is for . . .

United States Marine Hospital

Located on Portland Avenue in Louisville, the hospital opened in 1851 to serve civilian rivermen.

Upton

This small town in Hardin and Larue counties was named for himself by George Washington Upton.

V is for . . .

Vanceburg
The seat of Lewis County has one of Kentucky's few Civil War monuments to the Union cause.

Versailles

The seat of Woodford County was named in honor of the birthplace of the Marquis de Lafayette.

Villa Madonna College

Established in Covington in 1921, it became Thomas More College in 1968 and moved to a new campus in Fort Mitchell.

VILLA MADONNA COLLEGE AND ACADEMY
Main Building

W is for . . .

Warsaw
The Ohio River town, seat of Gallatin County, was named for an 1803 novel about Poland, *Thaddeus of Warsaw.*

Washington
This Mason County town is now a suburb of Maysville. Confederate General Albert Sidney Johnston was born here in 1803.

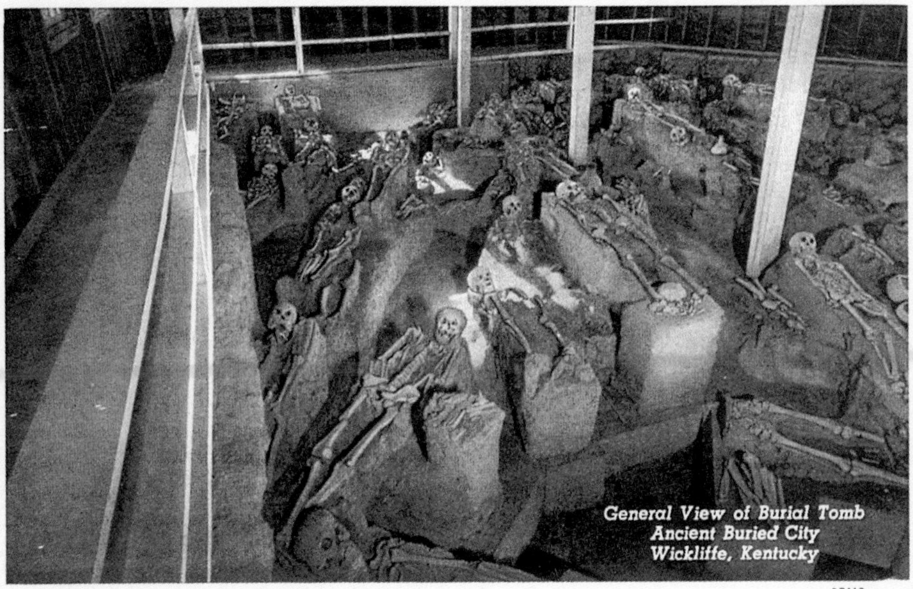

General View of Burial Tomb
Ancient Buried City
Wickliffe, Kentucky

9B110

Wickliffe

The Wickliffe Mounds, on the bluffs of the Mississippi in Ballard County and now under the jurisdiction of Murray State University, mark the burial grounds of a village of American Indians dating back to about 1,000 A.D.

Wilderness Road

Pioneers entering Kentucky through Cumberland Gap followed this route to settlements in the Bluegrass.

Old Wilderness Road at High Bridge, Ky.

Williamsburg

The seat of Whitley County, on the Cumberland River, is now the home of Cumberland College.

Winchester

Like many places in Kentucky, the seat of Clark County was named for a town in Virginia.

X is for . . .

The Spot

X marks the spot—where Governor William Goebel was mortally wounded by an assassin on January 30, 1900, on the front lawn of the Kentucky Capitol . . .

. . . and the motel room in Middlesboro where an anonymous traveler spent a night in the 1940s.

St. Xavier High School ("College")

Founded in 1864 on Broadway in downtown Louisville, the school moved to Poplar Level Road in 1961.

Y is for . . .

Yamacraw

This coal town in McCreary County, now almost nonexistent, was named for a tribe of Creek Indians.

Enid Yandell

The nationally known Louisville sculptor created the Hogan Fountain and the Daniel Boone statue in Louisville's Cherokee Park.

Z is for . . .

Zachary Taylor Home, Louisville, Ky.

Zachary "Old Rough and Ready" Taylor

The twelfth president's Louisville home, Springfield, adjoins the Zachary Taylor National Cemetery, where he is buried—except when his remains are removed for tests (as they were in 1991) to determine whether his mysterious death was the work of a nefarious poisoner. (It wasn't.)

ZACHARY TAYLOR MONUMENT, LOUISVILLE, KY.

From A to Z . . .

Kentuckians are proud of their state. Even when they move away, they remember who they are and where they came from, as attested by this March 1910 post card showing a gathering of transplanted Kentuckians in San Diego, California.

Index